Here and there

by Wil Ifan

with foreword by
David Prosser
Editor of *Western Mail*

WESTERN MAIL & ECHO LTD. CARDIFF

FOREWORD

IN this small volume are distilled in lovely prose the thoughts of an erudite mind and the emotions of a gentle spirit. Wil Ifan is distinguished as a poet in the Welsh language : in English he is a sweet-singing lyricist. As essayist he is the poet-philosopher, evoking from the commonplace the little joys and sorrows, hopes and fears that pattern the lives of simple people.

These essays and smaller pieces have all appeared in the *Western Mail* in Wil Ifan's weekly feature entitled " Here and There." They have been chosen and edited for this volume by his son, Brian Evans, who assuredly found it a labour of love to give durability to the work of so gracious a mind.

DAVID PROSSER

" Trash "

SOME knowledge of Welsh may materially aid one's understanding of English. After hearing a recent broadcast of " Tempest ", so complete was my satisfaction that it included the necessary germ of dissatisfaction. It drove me to the printed page again.

And there I came across this sentence, which I understood perfectly—until I read the explanatory note that went with it ! Said Shakespeare, " . . . who to advance and who to trash for overtopping. . . . "

The commentator says that here is a mixture of metaphors from hunting and gardening, for " to trash " is to fasten a weight on the neck of a dog to prevent his over-running his companions. This may be true, but to the countryman speaking Welsh, " trasho " is the word used to denote the very act of dealing with the over-topping branches of the hedgerow.

There are many similar instances where the English word that ventured across Offa's Dyke centuries ago has retained its original meaning, whereas the same word remaining on the wrong side of the Dyke has gradually changed it almost beyond recognition.

In London to-day a reader might well stumble over the Psalmist's use of the word " still " in " They will be still praising Thee," not realising that the word means " all the time " rather than " yet". But in Cardiganshire, if a farmer wanted to say (but he wouldn't), " It is always good weather for the harvest," he would exclaim, " Mae'n dywydd da *stil* adeg y cynhaeaf."

When a certain monoglot Englishman came to take charge of a school in Wales he was always puzzled when the village boys in their essays wrote of " doubting " a fire and " doubting " a candle He didn't realise that the good old English form " dout," first cousin to " doff " and " don," still lingered on their tongues though they didn't quite know how to spell it. In West Wales to this day they " tent " a screw and put up a " tilt " where you would " tighten " a screw and put up a " tent."

The capital of Wales

WHILE Cardiff, claiming to be the capital of Wales, was peeping over its shoulders to see how Swansea and the other villages were taking it, Tom Henblas placidly carried on with his task.

He was on top of a hedge on the climbing road to Synod Inn, Cardiganshire, lopping off the many ash-shoots and leaving just one sapling to be gashed deeply and then bent along the hedge.

It is remarkable how near to complete amputation this last operation may be ; but Tom's experienced axe knew that it always left just enough for the good sap to travel along, once the spring brings the turn of the tide.

The ash sapling, having meekly accepted its novel horizontal position, helped by the firm persuasion of Tom's knee and gloved hand, the thorn and the sycamore submitted to the same treatment.

" Bending the hedge " is South Cardiganshire's term for this annual operation, but Tom told me that a Tregaron man passing that way yesterday had called it not " plygu'r claw'," but " plethu'r berth," and so coastal and inland Cardiganshire between them have it right, for the complete operation is a combination of skilled bending and weaving—" plygu " and " plethu."

One realises that the busy commerce of town and city, the clatter of iron and steel, the whirr of great wheels above the valley coal-shafts, the loud debates of senate and council-chamber are all part and parcel of the body politic that we call Wales, but it is at our peril that we forget that Tom Henblas, who has never heard of us, is there in the January mist, intent on the age-long ritual of " bending the hedge."

The previous night I was one of a happy company in a chapel schoolroom above Llandyssul. There was a roaring fire in the open grate, and the ring of candles that hung from the ceiling shed a mellow light on faces that were at once interested and interesting.

Art, music, and literature were being discussed, and that, of course, in the unpolluted Welsh of Ceredigion.

I thought of them again as I watched Tom, for they, too, were " bending the hedge," which is the ultimate bulwark between the cultivated acres of the traditional Welsh life and the streaming traffic of so many new roads.

To get his perspective true every townsman ought to make an occasional excursion to the remote rural areas and that not in mid-summer but round about this season, when the fields are grey and the winding hedgerows the colour of ripe corduroy.

When we discuss the real wealth of the nation, be it from the material point of view or the moral and cultural, we may find that the true capital of Wales is in its little fields, guarded so diligently by Tom Henblas, and the men and women who meet in tiny candle-lit schoolrooms on hill and in dale.

22nd March, 1949

House-builders

THE boisterous March wind was not allowed to interfere with the building drive at the top of the trees. When a pair of crows have secured their " permit " they go on with the job irrespective of the weather, not even claiming double rate for working in the rain.

As I watched these two on their swaying scaffolding I couldn't help wondering whether they had definite knowledge that they were building a home for a family that was to be, or whether the gathering of sticks and all the noisy, busy weaving in a circular pattern was but blind instinctive urge, a restlessness that was merely part of the love-making.

One cannot answer, but it would surely be simpler to believe that they know exactly what they are up to. In any case, they go about things in a very businesslike way and have no truck with easy jerry-building methods.

A roadman who is my authority on birds and wild beasts, tells me that in his long experience of clearing the roads after mighty storms he has never known a crows' nest to be blown down. The nest only comes down when the tree comes down or the bough itself snaps ; so that, as a matter of fact, the popular nursery rhyme is nothing but an unsolicited testimonial to the old-established building firm of Messrs. Rook, Crow and Co. :

Rockaby, baby, on the tree-top,
When the wind blows the cradle will rock ;
When the bough breaks the cradle will fall
And down will come baby and cradle and all.

19th April, 1949

In the soup

IN the old days it was always refreshing to see the late Sir John Rowland sturdily treading Cardiff pavements into the mountain paths of Tregaron, and shouting his high-pitched greeting as if he were hailing a shepherd on a distant height.

One day I held him up to ask if he were going to correct some misleading newspaper report that appeared that morning.

" There are two sorts of people in the world " was his reply. " One sort flies to the Press to correct things, the other doesn't. I belong to the last lot."

And on the whole silence is just as well especially if the misleading report or the unfortunate misprint concerns yourself alone. And yet there are occasional slips and misprints that can give a man a very unhappy quarter of an hour.

I remember the occasion when in a painstaking sonnet I had sought to describe a Sunday morning at Newport ; the old castle ruins are there, the placid waters, and shattering the morning silence the dinning cars of the train crossing the bridge.

I could have wept the next morning when I saw the *dining-cars* that rattled over the ruins of my poor sonnet.

7

But in a review a book of poems of mine, rather foolishly entitled " The Songs of the Heather Heights," met with a still more unkindly fate. There it was in the boldest of bold-faced type : " The Soup of the Heather Heights " ; and all the kind things said in that review could not atone for the basin-ful at the head of the column.

The steam of that " soup " so clouded my glasses that I couldn't see clearly for days. But even then I withstood the temptation and remembered Sir John's chuckling dictum under the walls of Cardiff Castle.

10th May, 1949

Ann Griffiths

THOSE who visit Llanfyllin, in Montgomery, should make a point of seeing the old Congregational church there. It was the local grammar school head who read out for me the inscription high up over the door :

> " This Protestant chapel was rebuilt in the year of our Lord 1717, being the 172nd year since the Reformation, and the fourth year of the reign of King George."
> *Uno avulso, non deficit alter.*

I wonder whether the schoolmaster has used this inscription not only as an epitomised history lesson but also as a memorable example of Virgil's use of the Ablative Absolute.

The omission of an English translation is to be taken as a compliment to the reader's erudition, and I hope that he will not be unkind enough to suggest any other explanation !

I feel sure, however, that all the pupils are familiar with a later chapter in this chapel's long story, for it was here that Ann Griffiths, after hearing the preaching of the Rev. Benjamin Jones, of Pwllheli, resolved to give what remained of her young life to the singing of hymns that to this day are the choicest treasures of her country.

With an unconscious leaning towards the dramatic, most writers have painted in rather lurid hues the figure of the maid who entered that service. Having carefully studied most of the reliable sources, I must say that I see no foundation for such an assumption of worldliness.

All along she appears to have been a splendid type of young girl, fond of the pastimes of her day, and though not in sympathy with dissent, faithful to her own church. I feel that many other aspects of the story of the singer of Dolwar Fach call for further light.

The Amazon Bell

A T Port Talbot while I was meekly receiving my final instructions in the deacons' vestry before making for the pulpit I was rather perturbed to hear the insistent bell of a nearby church. "Don't look so worried," said a kindly elder, " that bell stops before you begin : it is the old Amazon bell."

I had no time to inquire further just then, but as soon as the service was over, before they had time to question me regarding my sermon, I questioned them about the Amazon.

Didn't I remember that terrific storm forty years ago when a sailing ship, which had only just left Port Talbot dock, was lost with forty of her crew ? Indeed, he who told me the tale had seen it all, and he could not forget the sight of the poor mariners perched aloft while the crowds on shore could only look on helplessly, for it was the worst gale in living memory.

And now the bell of the good ship Amazon which had measured out day and night for the sailors and clanged a way for them through many a fog, was piously doing duty for St. Agnes, measuring out new watches for her faithful people and, let us hope, helping them out in the fog. Later I lifted my eyes to see the old bell for myself and I could not but think of that final desperate clangour when wind and wave tolled the last watch for forty brave men.

The Little Towns

W HEN one reads of miners being stopped at one pit and directed to another one naturally sympathises with the inconvenience and the expense of the additional travelling involved. But there is one phase of the question that I had not previously considered. "Do you see," said one such displaced collier to me, "after over thirty years in one pit it's not an easy matter to find one's way about in another."

We super-terraneans forget that there is a whole township underground, with streets and lanes and junctions extending for miles, and in the endless night there are no convenient lamp posts to light up the names that aren't there !

But though no names are posted up the colliers themselves have christened each district and heading and parting. The National Coal Board, true to their love of order, have renamed the districts, using letters and numbers, office fashion, so that if you are not working in A 4 you may be in B 3 perhaps.

But my collier host spoke with nostalgic pride of the districts of his old pit, Ffynnon Dwym and Y Dduallt, Abyssinia and Shanghai. I wonder how long such names which are names can outlive the Coal Board's advancing regiments of mere letters and numbers?

12*th July*, 1949

Timothy Richard

WHEN a preacher talks of travelling in a Rolls-Royce you may be sure of two things : he himself is not sitting at the wheel, and he is wearing his clerical black. On this occasion, gliding along the road from Glamorgan to the top of Carmarthen, I was privileged to be next to the wheel, to hear the driver contrasting this journey with one he had undertaken years ago along this very road, when his wheel was a pair of reins.

He was then taking a party up from Caerau to Aberystwyth for a holiday. They had to put up for one night at Ammanford and another at Aberaeron, and on arrival the horse and he were put out to graze at Aberystwyth until the return journey ! To-day a Rolls-Royce does the same trip and back in an afternoon.

Anyone who knows the road from Ammanford to Lampeter can imagine what the country looks like this early July, with sunshine filtered through green leaves and the singing of birds.

There were trees all the way, but it was at Dynevor that they came to meet us in a solid phalanx. This must surely be one of the most overwhelmingly beautiful spots in the whole of Wales, the trees bearing down on you from the brow of the hill, while the very road beneath you is upheld by a rainbow of a bridge, a rainbow drained of all colour that you may concentrate on its perfect shape, and rebuilding itself in the glass of Towy, like Browning's thrush, " singing its song twice over."

One cannot dwell on all that was seen as we hurried by on that road. I knew the lane on our left that ended in Talyllychan Abbey, and the dreaming mere, but at the time my mind was too full of a roadside smithy that we had just passed.

For every one Welshman who knows the ruined abbey there is a score that cherishes that blacksmith's forge, for it was there that Thomas Lewis hammered out the hymn that is sung in hundreds of Welsh Communion services : and one need not apologise for using the hammer-and-anvil metaphor in referring to the composing of this hymn.

It may be crude in its workmanship, it may be hard in its theology, but it has certainly known the white heat of a fervent devotion.   It is a hymn about the cruel scourging that " ploughed up a back that was so fair," about the " nailing to a cross-beam ", about being " stricken down by His Father's sharp-edged sword ".

> *Wrth gofio'i riddfannau'n yr ardd,*
> *A'i chwys fel defnynnau o waed :*
> *Aredig ar gefn oedd mor hardd,*
> *A'i daro gan gleddyf ei Dad ;*
> *A'i arwain i Galfari Fryn*
> *A'i hoelio ar groesbren o'i fodd,*
> *Pa dafod all dewi am hyn ?*
> *Pa galon mor galed na thodd ?*

And at the very gate of Ffaldybrenin Churchyard there was another tiny smithy which bore a newly-placed tablet recording the fact that this dwelling, but not a smithy at the time, was the home of Timothy Richard, " Wales's gift to China."

It was Wales who gave China Griffith John and W. Hopkyn Rees, both great Christian missionaries ; but Timothy Richard was a missionary whose statesmanlike gifts materially helped to shape the destinies of that great land.   To think that this country lad, leaving the cottage at the chapel door, could have crossed the seas to win half a continent to a new way of life !

19th July, 1949

Pembroke's pillars

PEOPLE in South Pembrokeshire will scarcely believe me when I say that one day, from the top of a whinberry hedge above Whitland I had a view of Pembroke Dock ; but I confess it was an unusual view—just two solid pillars of black smoke holding up a sky that was sullen and ominous.

And those two pillars based on Pembroke Dock remained standing there solidly for many days, until at last the fire brigades of half Wales and beyond had controlled the burning oil-tanks and so demolished the terrible pillars.

Pembroke Dock still bears in its body the marks of that and many another scourging blitz and ordeal by fire.   It was rather pathetic to see the shell of what had once been a palatial business house still carrying in bold letters the familiar name of a great insurance company.

Evidently the company hadn't included a German blitz in its list of contingencies, but it can boast that it had, even in the holocaust, kept its good name !

Dolgellau

IF this is your first visit to Dolgellau I wonder what you think of it. " Town-planning " is a term of recent origin, but I sometimes imagine that those responsible for building this town on the banks of the Wnion were working according to plan, but that the plan was such an intricate one that the key to it can no longer be discovered.

I remember seeing one of the many English visitors who came to the town in the old days. She met me near Cambrian House and asked me in a straight, tired voice, " Can you please tell me the way to the country ? " And I thought that there was in her plea an echo of a plaintive appeal from " Pilgrim's Progress."

I could, of course, only ask her, putting as much sympathy as I could muster into my voice, " And where do you wish to go ? " And again, the same straight, tired voice, " Anywhere, please, out of the town. For the last half-hour I have been doing my best but I always find myself back here."

Yes, the dear old town is built like that ; those who do not know it can seldom find their way out ; those who know it never want to find their way out !

It is a town of one broad street and one and twenty narrow, lanes that can never quite make up their minds ; they may start out from the Square confidently making for the church or the market-hall or the Marian.

They look very business-like indeed and sure of their errand, but they have not gone many yards before they have met another pal of a lane and after a quiet chat they bear left or right as the whim takes them and though they still keep on going on you can tell that they have by now completely forgotten their errand and you are not surprised to see them bending back again to the Square to find out what it was.

As I said, there are one and twenty such lanes, each a bit uncertain and hazy but having its own personality and sense of humour. There will be tremendous Eisteddfod crowds in the broad street which we call a Square and some of us may occasionally wish to escape from our friends.

I shall be in a favoured position, as an escapist, for of the one and twenty lanes there is not a single lane whose secrets I do not know. Don't try to follow me for my trusty pals will only land you back in the Square again. They have a very keen sense of humour, and are very loyal to old friends.

If you ever find yourself unable to find yourself, spend the time in looking at the houses, I have never seen walls built of such mighty slabs of stone, and I cannot imagine how the masons hoisted these crags into position ; but then ten slabs or so would do for a whole wall, and they only needed to exert themselves to the full ten times or so whereas a normal wall would call for the trimming and dove-tailing of a hundred stones.

Those grey-to-black slabs which a band of masons could hardly lift into position are what you will take back with you to South Wales !

30th August, 1949

Ever new

COULD this happen outside Wales ? I know that it is one. like myself, who has never left home, who often asks such a question, giving a dogmatic negative implication as he does so. But at any rate I can vouch for the fact that it does happen here.

A bus starting out on its 15-mile climb into the mountains obligingly stopped to pick me up on the old bridge. I was the only passenger and the conductor almost before he had thumb-clicked my ticket asked me what I thought of the ancient Biblical Scrolls just discovered !

Making that dusty find his jumping-off point, he proceeded to deal with scriptural problems in general. He believed that the churches were no longer well attended because the pulpit was so uncertain in its pronouncements. Occasionally, between the Garden of Eden and the Pauline Epistles, he had to step off the bus to deliver a parcel ; sometimes he handed a passenger a ticket, but he never failed to return to the fray, carrying on his argument from the very point where he had dropped it.

During these temporary lulls I would look round to see the streams and the mountains, but I could hardly expect them to interest him for he had seen them six times a week for the last twenty-six years ; it was only his Bible that remained ever new to him.

August, 1949

Pyramid of pines

A MAN counting on a holiday at the seaside and dreaming of a glorious expanse of water in front of his bedroom window would be ill-advised to book his rooms on the mere evidence of the advertiser's " Sea-View," but when I arrived at " Pine Mount," Trefriw, whither I had been invited for a week-end, I found to my delight that it " answered to its name," if I may quote the jargon of the " Lost and Found " column.

Trefriw is within a mile of Llanrwst and it is a mile of enchantment. Afterwards there was a little climb that brought me to a footbridge spanning a ravine. I wanted to lean over the handrail to peep at the stream in the depths below, but my knees wouldn't let me !

Then again a climb to red-roofed " Pine Mount " nestling in a very paradise of trees. Did I say red ? The real roof was a green mountain of pines stretching up almost perpendicularly. As I looked at those countless trees standing on each other's shoulders I remembered " Yr Urdd's " gymnastic pyramids, only that here at Trefriw the topmost lad in green, instead of holding his arms out horizontally to retain his balance, flung them up to the sky in sheer exultation.

Whenever I am deeply moved by a view of land or water I find myself speaking of the place as the most beautiful spot in Wales. Trefriw is certainly one of them. Indeed I was tempted to say that is was the *most* " most beautiful," even though I had just arrived from Dolgellau and that via Trawsfynydd and Maentwrog and the steel-grey fastness of Ffestiniog, down through Bettws-y-Coed.

If a beauty-spot plebiscite were organised it is more than likely that Bettws-y-Coed would be at the very top of the poll, though I remember hearing of a bus-load of Lancashire trippers halting near Henllan Bridge on the River Teifi when one of the enthusiastic crowd was seen to wave his arms at the general scene, with a defiant challenge—" Where's your Betsy now ? "

However, I refuse to be drawn into a quarrel as to the rival charms of " Betsy Code " and Trefriw, for they are next-door neighbours.

I spent a sun-soaked hour on the river bank near the famed Llanrwst Bridge and as I looked at its lines I felt certain that Inigo Jones, whether he built it or not, would not be at all eager to scotch the tradition that it is his work.

6th September, 1949

All change

FEW are the things that abide. On one occasion when we were approaching Dolwar Fach, the home of Ann Griffiths, the hymn-writer, I asked the present tenant whether he thought there had been much change in the fields and lanes around.

His answer I think was fairly sound : " No, the nearer you get to nature the less likely are you to find much change," and so I knew still greater satisfaction in the thought that my eyes were resting on the very scenes that had met her wistful gaze day by day.

And yet, even in the heart of the country, though the lanes remain the ways of men may change.

I do not know who decreed it in the beginning, but as far back as men remember, Crymych Fair has been held on the last Tuesday of August. I should not like the deacons to believe that I had accepted an engagement at Whitland for the previous Monday just to be there in good time for the fair !

In the old days, Crymych Fair was considered to be one of gigantic importance ; indeed, it was altogether too big for youngsters like ourselves to venture there. But we, too, were privileged to sally forth in the late evening to meet the venturesome people who had actually attended and to receive at their hands an occasional fairing, in the way of fruit or sweets, or, as great a treat as any, a glorious bun shaped like a highwayman's hat.

I know that what you get at the shop to-day, its sogginess all puffed up and varnished over with pretence, is called " a bun," but please do not think of that at all when I speak of the fairing that Farmer John Hughes, stooping from the high throne of his dog-cart, handed to us when we met him at the top of Havod Lane to open the gates for him.

Things had changed this year ; reins had given place to steering wheels, and through the steaming fragrance of the sliced potato I could see no three-cornered pieces of sugar, currants and romance.

Hoop-la, coconut shies, and all the dizzying, screaming whirligigs that had ever been devised were there. It was a far more prosperous crowd to-day, and no-one there had heard of an ancient copper coin called a penny ; sixpence seemed to be the lowest denomination recognised at any stall.

The only thing that remained was the zest of young and old faces now lit up white in the glare of electricity under the shadow of Y Frenni Fawr, who seemed to be the only other fellow present who was remembering things.

20th September, 1949

Fabulous Guto

THERE was great excitement round about Laleston a few years ago when Arthur Morgan won the " Powderhall," and those of us who had been privileged to see him training for the race were especially pleased with the result.

The news reel, when it was shown locally, commanded a crowded house, and there was almost a cathedral hush when the hero was shown getting ready, and the ejaculation of one overwrought woman sounded more like a prayer than anything else : " I do hope Arthur will win ! " forgetting for the instant that her prayer had already been answered.

Guto Nyth Brân ran his fabulous Powderhalls and Marathons before the film era ; neither were there any stop-watches about, but this young runner from the parish of Llanwynno could certainly move if half the tales about him are true or, indeed, if any of the tales are half-true.

He had taken more time than usual in rounding the mountain sheep, but when he was reprimanded for not having taken the dog to help him, he explained : " I had no difficulty with our sheep, but that brown lamb over there gave me no end of a run ! " The lamb was a mountain hare that by now looked far more tired than Guto !

4th October, 1949
Great and small

A HUMOROUS travel book, " Westward Ha ! " has for its sub-title " Around the World in Eighty Clichés." As everyone knows, Wynford Vaughan Thomas, who has now divided the eighty by ten, has certainly carried no " clichés " around with him. That was the most marked feature of his day-to-day chronicles, at once breathless and breath-taking.

He is the sort of narrator who can't possibly repeat what others have said because his eyes are forever seeing things for the first time ; and even when he is visiting a place for the second time, since he always brings a new pair of eyes along with him, that too, is a surprise and an excitement.

Some of us live in smaller worlds, a tapestried world of parishes, but they, too, can be interesting. I remember talking to a man outside an institution for old people at Dolgellau.

I wondered whether he had travelled much in his younger days and his reply had about it a suggestion of pride in his adventurous youth. " Well, yes, I have been more than once within sight of Towyn." And coming " *I olwg Tywyn* " beyond the mighty mountain ranges may have been for him as soul stirring as Keats imagined it must have been for " stout Cortez . . . Silent upon a peak in Darien."

A similar memory takes me back to a road in Pembrokeshire. The farmer driving the car had persuaded his wife to come with him. Her illness had for years confined her to the house and he took great delight in pointing everything out to her.

Though we were only a few miles from her home all was new territory to her and I heard her whisper : " *'Rwyt ti, John, wedi gweld llawer mwy o'r byd na* fi ! " (You, John, have seen much more of the world than I).

I shouldn't be surprised to hear that Wynford Vaughan Thomas after being whirled round the globe in eight days is rather envious of the man whose five continents are five parishes and whose airliner is a rumbling cart on a country lane.

The decoy rose

I HAVE no wish that this note should give rise to learned botanical disquisitions in the correspondence columns, and I am certainly not prepared to answer sceptical questions. I simply supply the bare chronicle.

One day I picked up on the pavement an artificial pink rose ; the texture and colour of the petals were life-like, but the perfume was, to say the least, a little extravagant. I hadn't the heart to throw the rose into the gutter, and yet I couldn't very well put it in the lapel of my coat ; the deacons might have considered it rather big, and if they came within range they might well have resented the effeminate perfume, or perhaps succumbed to it.

I thrust it into my pocket for I knew exactly what to do with it. Our rambler bush that had shown wonderful blooms right through the long summer was now without a single rose. What would be easier than to fix this splendid work of art on its lapel, and so cheer up the prickly, poverty-stricken fellow who had done so well for me since early June ? It didn't take me two minutes.

Not the following day, but the day after, believe it or not, two genuine roses burst forth in full bloom, one directly above the decoy rose, and the other to the left of it ; they were just as beautiful, though, I must confess, their delicate scent could not compete with the overwhelming, all-conquering perfume of my pavement rose.

25th October, 1949

Shadows

A FAMILY in South Cardiganshire had recently moved from one farm to another and one expected to find them very happy in their new home, and indeed all had gone well, but for one thing. They complained that the kitchen was no longer the same, though they had retained every article of furniture.

" We have the old dresser in the very same position, and we have tried the table lamp in all sorts of positions, but we can't get it back."

Do you know what they had lost ? In the old kitchen, as soon as the lamp was lit, there was an unmistakable picture above the fire place. It was the shadow face of their old minister. " We have shifted the dresser, we have moved the table, we have raised the lamp, but we have lost him forever now, and our home will never be the same."

17

I know that water reflections are shadows only in the sense that they are insubstantial. I think it was Walter Map who told the tale of a king who felt aggrieved because one of his courtiers had dreamed about the queen and had been foolish enough to tell his dream to somebody.

The king, stung to the quick by the imagined insult, laid the matter before the judge, who pronounced judgment as follows : The offending courtier was to take his herd of cows to the banks of Llangorse Lake and walk them in single file along the water's edge. The king was to be allowed to do what he liked with the " shadows "!

If readers should care to have all the details right they must turn to Dr. R. T. Jenkins's book on Walter Map, but the bare story as it stands furnishes us with a rare example of the dispensing of poetical justice where an imagined insult is cleared by an imagined penalty ; a shadow to pay for a shadow.

8th November, 1949

Diplomats

I RECENTLY met two budding diplomats at a breakfast table. Though they were both under three years of age they clearly had the root of the matter in them. Said the mother to the boy : " Stop it ! You mustn't kick the table like that ! " And then came the answer which in persuasive tone and meek deliberation sounded quite convincing, " I am not kicking the table : I am only smacking it with my feet."

The girl's excuse for not eating her porridge was that it was too hot and that she wanted it cooled. In this case it was the thoughtful father who volunteered to cool it for her with some more milk, " No, dad, please, I want you to cool it with some more sugar."

There we have two main principles of diplomacy exemplified: the art of making a thing seem different by a skilful manipulation of the terms describing it ; and then a wholehearted confidence in the universal efficacy of a few grains of sugar, even when it comes to cooling a plateful of hot porridge.

Such early wisdom at a square breakfast table must surely end at some round table or other.

6th December, 1949

People of the Vale

DESPITE the winds and rains of early winter there are days when one can venture abroad ; but once out, a cross-road puzzle is often more difficult to solve than a crossword puzzle.

Not that one doesn't know the way. Both roads may be familiar, and both may be good, indeed so good that one cannot decide which to reject.

How often have I hesitated, as I do to-day, when Merthyr Mawr and Ewenny are beckoning at the same time. On this occasion it was Ewenny that won and I soon forgot Merthyr Mawr as I went along happily.

It was my happy mood, perhaps, that added a little too much vigour to my " Hullo ! " as I greeted a carter who was coming to meet me. His horse stopped dead at the sound of my voice and I fear that the good man at his head took quite a time to persuade him that the last syllable " —ô " was not a variant of " wo ! "

I smiled as I remembered how many of us on the road are quite prepared to accept every greeting as a sufficient excuse for taking a breather.

Those who know birds and their ways would perhaps have found nothing strange in the way in which a hawk behaved that morning. But I had never before seen it flying so methodically and slowly along hedge after hedge, almost skimming the top twigs, and occasionally alighting for a second or two.

One knows that a hawk must live, but I wished that I had not seen it at a time when the whole world seemed so restful and unsuspecting.

Another day found me on the mountain slope above Llanharan, where a young farmer talked enthusiastically of the thrill of converting rough mountain land into green fields and I saw with amazement how, with only a wall between, the rich grassland lived next door to the rusty fern.

But the dry built wall was a solid one, aided by a system of barbed wiring that would have satisfied the commandant of a concentration camp. He spoke of the wily mountain sheep who would walk down for hundreds of yards to a gap in the wire defences on their side of the wall and then along the top of the wall for hundreds of yards until they found an accommodating gap in the wire on the other side.

Then he quoted with ironic accents :
  " For what are men better than sheep or goats,
  That nourish a blind life within the brain."

" A blind life within the brain ? " " No," he added ; " Tennyson was evidently not a mountain farmer ! "

It was no surprise for me to hear this farmer quoting Tennyson. I knew that his wife, too, had been college trained, but that she had found her heart's delight in the open air and especially in tending the mountain sheep.

Indeed, she is considered to be one of the most efficient shepherds in the district. As her husband confessed with pride, " I can *count* sheep as well as the next, but she *knows* them "— which is the " higher mathematics " of shepherding.

If you went into the living-room of the old farmhouse you would see a water colour stuck on the distempered wall and a bardic chair in the parlour, both picture and chair proclaiming the artistic bent of the shepherdess's sister.

That evening I listened to two sisters singing and playing Mendelssohn, the poet sitting at the piano while her sister joined her in the singing of " O, Lovely Peace."

I was charmed not only by the steady voices but almost as much by the steadiness of the hand that held that heavy table-lamp. It was no wonder that its owner had such a firm grip on the rein of her mettlesome mountain pony.

31st January, 1950

'Eight into four'

TO-DAY, any man who succeeds in finding a suitable flat ought to " thank whatever gods there be." And yet a flat, however self-contained and self-satisfied, is not a house ; and when one tries to put what filled eight rooms into four the old " standard one " formula sings in one's brain, " Eight into four won't go."

A kindly neighbour begged me not to worry ; that after a few months in the new place I should become quite flat-minded. " Flat-minded," but that is almost as bad as being flat-footed !

" Eight into four won't go," which means parting with many things, and the more old and valueless they are the more difficult it is to wish them good-bye.

If anyone had come across this pile of Cymanfa Ganu programmes he might well imagine that I had spent a lifetime doing nothing but singing hymns. I wonder how many would have guessed the identity of the accompanist on this Newport programme.

Surely, " Miss May Jones, L.R.A.M.," must be the Mai Jones who has just taken Thomas of the many Troubles to cheer the heart of London Town. Though she has long been an organist at the Welsh chapel in Newport, I believe that she was born in the same town as a musician of an earlier age, Pencerdd Gwalia. That is why perhaps I always feel that Mai Jones's piano playing is a near approach to harp playing at its best. You listen again.

Virtuoso

I HAVE long been a grateful admirer of the man who can play the piano really well, getting those dots and lines into the brain and on to the finger-tips, and thence to the black and white keys that unlock the gates of paradise.

But recently, though I am not of a fickle nature, my admiration has wavered from the piano-player to the piano-shifter.

Though he is a man of mightier arms and shoulders than the musician, he too, is a virtuoso. He, too, seems to be reading a definite score that is invisible to less keen-eyed mortals.

I should like you to have seen him and his mate at the foot of that stairs, with its tricky hairpin bend.

He was giving preliminary instructions to the other mate half-way up the stairs. As he interpreted the score his words uttered in a very low voice were few and short, but his hands never stopped talking.

Every contemplated move and turn were built first of all in the air with those eloquent hands of his.

I remembered watching Pachmann talking and making familiar magical passes, building his airy castle before he bowed his broad back to lay the first stone.

All three pianists had now understood the plan of campaign to a turn, and then came the actual recital ; every movement was perfectly co-ordinated, and though there were bursts of super-human energy they kept a strict tempo, and the rests at every third step were duly observed.

But that hairpin bend. It seemed unnegotiable. It was when they came to that stage that I understood the significance of those preliminary passes at the foot of the stairs.

The obedient piano, like a polished performing bear, was made to stand on its hind legs.

It wagged its head this way and that way. It gracefully kicked its heels in the air, and regaining its balance, at last climbed the five remaining steps and walked triumphantly into the room.

Pachmann, at the end of his recital in the old Cardiff Empire received a thunder of handclaps, but those three panting men expected no plaudits.

For them it was just a job of work. Henceforth my piano will want to honour two types of musicians, the man who can play it and the man who can shift it.

And which of the twain is the greater artist I do not know.

Tunnels

WHICH is the longest railway tunnel in Wales ? I should think that the " Rhondda and Swansea Bay " possesses one long stretch of midnight that might figure well in the competition. You are plunged in at Blaen Cwm Rhondda, and are only released when the day breaks upon you at Blaen Gwynfi, or the " Cape of Good Hope," as we called the place in the old days.

I was a lone passenger and glad enough of the electric lamp that helped to dispel the gloomy thought of being right under a big mountain.

It was hereabout that I once descended a pit and knew the same sort of feeling of having too much of the world on top of me.

As the fireman and I picked our way along those narrow lanes of the under-world I could sympathise with sweating men who had literally to " pick " their way along.

The black road from Blaen Cwm to the Cape was long enough to give me ample time to think of other tunnels. I remembered the vivid description given by the late Jennie Maitland of the long series of pigmy tunnels that play a game with you when you have left the junction and are making for Aberdyfi. She felt that she was running along the dark funnel of a flute that was punctured by little holes of sunshine.

I was once in a long tunnel with the late Dr. Peter Price. We had left Carmarthen, and a mart-day Carmarthen, with a full complement of farmers. If you knew Peter Price you would know that it only took him two minutes to be on friendly and enthusiastic terms with all of us. In the middle of his hearty handshaking and tense inquiries about market prices and what not I butted in :

" You all know who he is ; he is going to lecture to-night at Llandyssul ; at this rate he will wear himself out before he arrives at the pulpit. Now instead of allowing him to talk about the weather and the mart I suggest that we ask him to give us to-night's lecture so that we can all profit by our journey."

When the learned Doctor saw how my suggestion was received, like a big obedient child he took down his bag from the rack and we were soon listening spellbound. At Bronwydd Arms, at Cynwyl and at Pumpsaint some passengers had to stop off, but the lecturer's flowing eloquence did not cease and you ought to have seen the outgoing farmers on the platform hanging on to his words to the very last, with a hand on the carriage window.

We were still a fair number when the train entered the tunnel at Pencader, but as it was unlit the lecturer had to halt, and I think he quite appreciated my remark before he restarted : " I never knew before that this was such a long tunnel ! "

The " Rhondda and Swansea Bay " may hold the record in actual yards, but the Pencader tunnel can be a good second, when it holds up the eloquence of a Peter Price.

28th March, 1950

At Brynmawr

I COULD hardly believe it, but when I arrived in Brynmawr there wasn't a sign of snow anywhere, not on the mountain tops, even ! On many a previous visit I had received a cold, white welcome, and though Monmouthshire was blinking in the bright March sunshine I feared that Brynmawr would want to show me once again what it could do in the way of imitating Switzerland.

But even without its snow it was unmistakably Brynmawr. Where else would you find shaggy mountain-ponies nosing around unconcernedly in the town square ?

I stopped to watch a fine specimen which I met near the station. He was hanging round a chip-shop, and before long a young man came from the counter and was soon sharing the delicious delicacy with his pal from the mountains.

I wasn't quite near enough to know whether the pony complained that the savoury morsels were rather hot or to hear him saying he would like a little more vinegar on them.

4th April, 1950

Spring scene

IT isn't likely that the crows know anything about correspondence columns, and it may have been only my idea that they seemed rather self-conscious as they swooped round a tiny flock of sheep and lambs on Cefn Hirgoed.

So as not to be drawn into the controversy I avoid being too definite in my designation, for " crows " may do duty for ravens, rooks and jack-daws. Had these Cefn Hirgoed birds read the papers they would know that they are on the one hand suspected of killing lambs and blinding ewes and championed on the other as being the farmer's best friends.

They gathered round, but the dozing adult-members of the flock didn't seem to mind, and the lambs playfully swerved like white-jerseyed threequarters when one of the all-blacks flew too near.

I had ample time to watch the game, but when I saw one crow making off with a long skein of wool I took it for granted that there was nothing more sinister in the proceedings than a desire to have nests more cosily upholstered than usual.

And I always had an idea that a crow was satisfied with the plain basket-work of twigs !

When I went away a humorous old ewe, heedless of bad grammar, was teaching two lambs a new nursery rhyme :

> " Caw ! Caw ! Black thief,
> Have you stole my wool ? "
> " Yes, sir, yes, sir,
> Three beaks full."

The lambs that I saw a few days later on the golf links at Aberystwyth—not that I am a golfer—were not a whit more lively than the Cefn Hirgoed youngsters, but their games were better organised. They would line up and start a flying down-hill gallop, jumping the hurdles in fine style and photo-finishing in a bunch past the red flag.

I thought it very kind of the groundsmen to have troubled to erect all those hazard dykes just to please a lot of spring lambs, who, for all I know, were not even members.

11th April, 1950

Wringing of the heart

" GRAY'S Elegy written in a Crematorium " ; no, that would be an impossible title. In that " Country Churchyard " many centuries lay buried, and local family names could be traced far back until they were at last rubbed out by the weather or covered by the stone-moss. But here all is new, for cremating is itself new : all is new and up-to-date.

Yet, knowing all this, as I stood there to pay silent tribute to a firm friend, I felt that a new Gray could write just as effective an elegy in this new place. For death itself is very old ; the wringing of the heart, the stupefying sense of loss are older than crumbling stone.

Rhys Richards was just one of the thousands of Rhondda colliers who had brought " the country " up with them to the Glamorgan mines, and beneath the sunny, rollicking fun which is God's antidote to the pit's long corridors of midnight there remained to the end the sober regard for religion and spiritual culture.

It was here, too, just a few weeks ago, that they brought the body of Edward Thorogood Keep, of Hirwaun. His short life-story was a romance of high endeavour that brooked no hindrance from the day when he was brought to Bridgend's School for the Blind as a tiny lad, a bundle of mischief and cleverness. Indeed, the broadcast featuring the achievements of this great school and its great principal was written round the career of Eddie Keep.

From Bridgend he went to Worcester College for the Blind, and thence to the University College at Swansea. There he " worked and sang " all the week, and preached and sang on Sunday.

Not satisfied with a first-class honours degree in philosophy, he wrote a thesis that gained him his M.A. It was a bitter disappointment for one who revelled in scholarship that because of his blindness no fitting place could be found for him in school or college.

And now when I think of the brilliant boy who remained a bundle of mischief to the end, I must add a new placename to the list, Hirwaun, Bridgend, Worcester, Swansea—and Glyntaf.

Already have many sorrowing hearts written their elegies in a crematorium.

25th April, 1950

Ghosts

LAST Sunday morning, going to my publication—(Why is a preacher's engagement called his " publication " ?)—I had as fellow-travellers in the bus the Rev. William Henry, Gwilym Hiraethog, and Dr. Thomas Rees, of Swansea.

The conductor didn't ask Hiraethog and Dr. Rees for their tickets ; he passed them by as if they were not there at all, but he gave Mr. Henry his return to Nantymoel (one and four) and he knocked a penny off mine because I was only going as far as Ogmore Vale.

It was Mr. Henry, 85 years of age and still going strong, who had brought the other two along with him. They had been preaching at the opening services of New Siloh at Glandwr, where William Henry, then a young ministerial student at Swansea, had heard them and had never forgotten.

I almost heard Hiraethog chuckle as Mr. Henry vividly described how the two giants had almost wrestled for the pulpit Bible when the congregation was singing the last hymn before the first sermon.

Neither wanted the onus of delivering the second sermon for each knew that it would require much courage to follow when the people had already been moved by a great oration.

It was Dr. Rees who won, and though Rees was a mighty man of valour in the pulpit and had preached tremendously, Hiraethog, too, even as he read his text, was immediately master of the assembly.

And the Rev. William Henry repeated that text for me, intoning it as Hiraethog did, nodding his head to accent certain syllables and half-unconsciously closing one eye (Hiraethog, like Christmas Evans, had lost an eye)—*Bywhâ fi, O Arglwydd, yn ôl dy air.*

Neither the bus conductor nor the passengers knew that we were carrying Hiraethog and Dr. Rees with us that morning, but I knew it, and I am hoping that my congregation, too, knew at one remove the contagion of the fervent spirit of two giants from another age.

30*th May*, 1950

Parallels

NOBODY can pass Kilgetty on the way to Tenby without seeing the camp of caravans ; and they are the genuine article ; not your bijou, white-enamelled palace on wheels trailing behind a glossy car.

The grazing horses scattered over the moor are also there, ready to hand if and when these caravans think of moving. And these horses, too, are the genuine gipsy article. I had never before asked myself why a caravanner likes a pied horse. Is it because the while patches will help him to find his beast on a dark night in these hedgeless moors ?

Few men will visit Tenby without seeing this camp, but how many seeing the camp will also see Tenby's greatest son, Augustus John ? One recognises gladly that Tenby, with its golden wealth of colour, may have had much to do with inspiring Britain's greatest painter, but I like to think that he owes even more to Kilgetty, that it is the caravan that set his blood coursing and not the palatial boarding-houses on the cliffs.

From the very first, in his art, he seems to have turned his scornful back on the placid sea and climbed to the brown, bleak stretches of Kilgetty where the colourful men, women and children have no kinship with England or Wales, seeking no abiding city, but for generations building their homes on the romantic foundation of four wheels.

Did I say " the greatest son " ? When I turned into the parish church at Tenby, rich with many mellowed memorials, I read beneath a carved stone head these words :

> In memory of Robert Recorde, the eminent mathematician, who was born at Tenby Circa 1510. To his genius we owe the earliest important English treatise on algebra, arithmetic, astronomy, and geometry. He also invented the sign of equality $=$ now universally adopted by the civilised world. Robert Recorde was Court physician to King Edward VI and Queen Mary. He died in London 1558.

And Augustus John will not mind if I now revise or qualify my claim on his behalf, for strange as it may seem the artist and the mathematician share honours here. And perhaps we have been too prone to imagine that they ought to stand apart. Is it just a coincidence that so many musicians are also great mathematicians ? Is there truth in the remark that Bach's fugues have a pattern that is mathematically correct ?

Leonardo da Vinci, the outstanding Italian artist, was also the outstanding practical scientist of his day and generation, and it is possible that mathematics and artistry when they have both travelled far enough merge gradually the one into the other, and it will seem quite natural that Augustus John will at some distant day be commemorated in the same hallowed corner as Robert Recorde, who " invented the sign of equality $=$ now universally adopted by the civilised world."

And doesn't this last sentence go singing along beyond mathematics and beyond artistry to the realm of fundamental human relationships ? What Robert Recorde said in two short lines, one superimposed on the other, Abraham Lincoln eloquently enlarged into the ringing rhetoric of a memorable Presidential address—

> " Four score and seven years ago our fathers brought forth on this Continent a new nation, conceived in liberty, and dedicated to the proposition that all men are created equal."

It is never enough to employ the plus sign between man and man, just adding them together, and thinking of a people merely as an answer to that addition sum. In the last resort artists and mathematicians, rich and poor, black and white, rulers and people will only truly find themselves when two short parallel straight lines, linking man to man, will be " universally adopted by the civilised world."

Blue heights

THE bluebell-covered hillocks of Pembrokeshire looked like—what do you think ? No, not anything as poetical as you would expect from the county of magic—they looked in the distance very much like the coaltips of Glamorgan, where the blue of the rubble has not been carpeted over by the young, forgiving green.

And yet when a few days later I found myself hemmed in by the actual tips above Dinas and Penygraig I found it very hard indeed to believe that there are such things in the world as gently undulating hills of bluebells.

On the Whit-Monday, and even on the Sunday, scores of children scrambled up the hillside to the foot of these forbidding bluebell heaps of the Rhondda Valley, and because they are true children of the Rhondda, irrepressibly adventurous and gay, perhaps they found what they sought, even though there were no flowers about.

Those who revel in Huw Menai's phantasies and who rejoice that the State considers it an honour to keep a poet going should remember that these are his hills : on these barren heights it is no wonder that he has to play the creator and fashion petals for himself.

But then the cuckoo-call from Trealaw has no coaldust on it and the stars above Penygraig are just as bright as those above the seven cantrefi of Dyfed—brighter perhaps because Huw Menai is looking at them.

The children had climbed the hills, and I expect it was in a spirit of give and take that the lambs came down to spend their Whit-Monday on the streets.

They must have been feeling very much at home there for they hardly took any notice of the many dogs on the pavement, though a mother sheep would now and then stare scoldingly at the terrier who was trying it on with one of the youngsters.

I was told that these sheep have quite a keen traffic sense—as pedestrians go, and from that grudging, qualifying clause you will have already guessed that my informant was a motorist !

" One thing you can be sure of," he gratefully added, " is that a sheep will always dash in the direction that its face is turned ; it won't change its mind suddenly and turn back."

I shouldn't like motorists to accept that as a general statement of fact and act on it, for it may only apply to Trealaw and Tony-pandy where men and sheep alike seem to know their own minds.

Two sons

YOU would hardly charge one with eavesdropping when the lady who sat in the corner of the compartment was talking at the top of her voice. Each hand, too, was talking at the top of its voice, every eloquent gesture adding new meaning to her words.

As a matter of fact when I entered the carriage I had fully meant to carry on with the crossword puzzle which I had started on a platform seat " as waiting " for my train : and before I go further I must ask you to relish that " as waiting," for I have been enjoying Jack Jones's " Give me Back My Heart," where this Welsh English construction recurs time and again.

But Jack mustn't think that it is his copyright, for I remember coming across it on many a page of the " Funeral Orations " delivered by the learned Samuel Roberts, A.M., of Llanbrynmair.

As it was, I did not take the paper out of my pocket again, for he is a foolish man who will glue his mind on the printed word when the air is full of good talk.

I felt sure that the speaker in ordinary circumstances was a softly spoken woman, but she was now trying to carry on a conversation with two people who had very little English, a young man and a young woman from Sweden.

And understandably enough we English speakers lift up our voices when addressing foreigners, unconsciously drawing a false analogy with our difficulty in making the rather deaf understand. It is easier than learning a new language, but scarcely as effective !

In this case, however, the woman from Swansea way, her finely-chiselled features and her wavy, dark hair contrasting sharply with the round faces and flaxen hair of her Swedish friends, did manage to get a great deal across the high bridge of her voice supported by the flying buttresses of two hands.

But she had chosen a difficult topic. If you wanted to describe the cockle-fishing of Penclawdd, and your eager listeners hadn't the remotest idea what " cockle " meant, how would you go about it ?

Like so many of us she was fond of rounding off her sentences with the ornamental " Do you see ? " worn down by much use to the single word " —see ? " Even this could be rather bewildering to alien ears—" a sort of shell-fish in the sea, see."

And the " donkeys," too, were most unmanageable ! " You know what I mean, a little horse, like " ; and with a careful horizontal open-palmed hand she measured their height in the air.

It was a good game and the two laughing Swedes who were bound for Gorseinon understood at last that there was a luscious feast awaiting them if they called at the Swansea Market on the morrow.

And then came a dramatic turn. The lady's son is a renowned footballer belonging to the most famous of all English soccer teams. He had played on the Continent ; yes, in Sweden : and, if I understood the excited Swede aright, he himself had seen the very game. And now chance acquaintanceship had become something much more ; photographs were shown, and the footballer's name and address were carefully written down.

Who would belittle the joyous pride of the mother when this bit of news was so unmistakably grasped ? It didn't matter so much now if the intricacies of cockle-fishing were still a bit hazy to the visitors.

And she had another son. And her voice dropped now. Even if the Swedes didn't understand, she knew that we two, one in each corner, were listening. And it was a story that couldn't be shouted, much less gesticulated over.

Before the war she had lived in a company house owned by a great German firm near Swansea. The director's wife gave birth to a boy near the time when her own boy was born. I think she said it was in the same house. At any rate the two boys grew up together, and the two mothers together watched over them.

Before the outbreak of war the German family returned to Germany. Her boy was killed flying over Berlin, the other killed flying over Britain.

No, I fear the flaxen-haired girl sitting next to me didn't quite understand, though her face was clouded with sympathy. It was hard to change the subject for we were all deeply moved.

The man from Kenfig Hill sitting opposite me was holding on his knee a little lad, Kenneth, the best-behaved Kenneth that I have ever known. I invited the little boy to look at the hundred pictures on the Swedish lady's dress, and when I asked him where I could buy a similar dress for my wife, there was much laughter, for because of my clerical collar they had visualised a staid little woman in black relieved possibly by an occasional discreet hint of white.

But the picture of a minister's wife going to the mothers' meeting in Swedish costume had accomplished what I wanted. The good mother from Swansea now regained her voice, and when the Kenfig Hill man and I left I am not sure that with deft hands she was not reopening the cockle-shells again.

Rabbits on the lawn

WHEN I saw a little girl picking dandelion leaves in the lane on the way home from school I knew immediately what it meant, and before she had time to feel shy I was asking her about the rabbit. " How old is it ? " She didn't know.

" It isn't a baby rabbit, is it ? " " Oh, no, it's about this size," placing the imaginary rabbit between her free hand and the hand that clutched the young leaves.

The colour was a " sort of brown like," and so I gathered it was an ordinary field rabbit. " We've only had him for about seven weeks ; father saved him when he was fighting a stoat."

Perhaps it was actually a weasel and not a stoat, but her phrase struck me as being a very graphic description of a certain kind of encounter : " a rabbit fighting a stoat."

Too often have we witnessed in the realm of men and affairs this pathetic unequal combat which, after all, is no combat.

The victim helplessly, with sheer sleep-walking movement, trying to flee, followed by the relentless pursuer who knows the end of the story from the first page. " Fighting " did you say ? But only as the rabbit fights the stoat.

I knew what the little girl was " up " to when she stooped to pick the leaves for I myself had often been on the same foraging expedition. It might surprise those who knew my father to learn that he ever allowed his children to keep rabbits ; he didn't believe in any kind of coop, and perhaps I ought to explain how it came about.

Somebody had caught two tiny rabbits in a field and had presented them to us. And this was the dilemma. To let two baby-rabbits loose in our world of coal-tips and slag heaps would mean certain death : to ask the would-be kind friend to take them back to where he found them was impossible.

So for some months they lived in and on our front lawn ; and never before, or since, have I seen employed that combined method of lawn-mowning and rabbit-rearing. The roomy house where they lived had its four walls and roof of wire netting, the floor, of course, being the lush grass.

Each day the house was moved-on a step, and so was the lawn kept down and the rabbits' morale kept up, my handfuls of foraged dandelions providing the necessary additional vitamins, vitamins that in those uneducated days had not yet learnt the alphabet.

And then when the rabbits were old enough to have a vote and to claim their liberty they were taken over Gwar-y-caeau, and let loose among the other brown denizens of Byass's fields above Aberavon.

31

The blue pyramid

TO go from the mining village where I stayed to a neighbouring mining village you cross a bridge and climb an incredibly stiff hill before you get to the open, high moorland that connects the two.

I naturally took my time on this hill and I wasn't surprised or ashamed when three women overtook me and passed on. For one thing I was older than they were, and I was on holiday. Why should I kill myself on the hill?

I hadn't expected the three women to slacken their pace to suit mine, but though I was a stranger, I did expect some sort of greeting, for here we are not slow to " Good morning ! " each other.

They didn't seem to see me. The middle girl looked ill and she was leaning rather on the arm of the older woman on her right. She held a handkerchief to her mouth, and I thought possibly she had been visiting a dentist.

But as I said, they climbed on and were soon out of sight ; but not completely out of my mind. However, on the open mountain stretch I didn't allow this incident, which I hoped was nothing serious, to destroy my happiness and I sat down to enjoy the morning that gloried over the land.

There, black against the east, was a cluster of trees sheltering a farmhouse, and when the eye took the road that ran across the moor one saw the inevitable blue pyramid of the distant colliery.

I couldn't quite guess how far it was for the eye is so accustomed to call blue " far " that it gets bewildered when it tries to remember that it may be just the blue of coal.

All I know is that the pyramid was no blot on the landscape ; it fitted into the picture perfectly and I am happy to think the little white streamer of smoke close by meant that there was work and life in that village of the pyramid.

The very next morning the newspaper had a tiny paragraph reporting a casualty to a native of that village—" Leslie Watkins, aged 26, a single man, was fatally injured by a fall of stone."

It was at another pit that he died, but he was brought home to the little village at the end of my road.

And then in the local paper another paragraph :

" Profound sympathy is felt for Miss Gwen Cooper, of Glanrhyd, whose fiancé, Mr. Leslie Watkins, was fatally injured in an accident at Brynteg Colliery."

Little did I realise that the brave young girl climbing that hill was ascending Via Dolorosa.

She was hurrying to comfort her lover's widowed mother at Crynant, widowed a few years previously at the foot of the same blue pyramid, widowed as the brave, beautiful climbing girl was now being widowed, a few weeks before her wedding day.

To comfort and be comforted.

One day I shall climb to that moorland again and I hope that I shall now better understand the message of the blue pyramid—on the Welsh landscape.

26th September, 1950

High wind

THERE is the old story of the farm labourer at the hiring fair who, when asked by a prospective employer as to his capabilities answered, " I can sleep soundly . . . " only to be sharply pulled up with, " But surely that is no testimonial ! " " You didn't let me finish, sir : I can sleep soundly on the stormiest night *when I've thatched the ricks*."

And the farmer at last understood that he was about to engage a man able to do his job so thoroughly in the rickyard that there need be no anxiety when the autumn and winter winds got going.

Few are the thatched ricks in Welsh yards this September, and even the few " safely gathered in " were the cause of much anxiety during the boisterous buffeting of the last week.

I happened to be in Prys-Jones's " Mountains of Glamorgan " just when one of the many storms was blowing itself out. A rueful glasshouse was lying down flat in the garden as if to avoid the onslaught, but even if it could ever find its feet again it would be useless as every pane was shattered.

But to go back to the ricks. In Cardiganshire, where people speak in parables, you will seldom hear conceit referred to directly and by name. Where you and I would say that Farmer So-and-So is a bombastic fellow, Cardiganshire mutters—" *Mae gormod o'r stwff 'na sy'n bwrw deisi lawr yndo fe* " : " He's got too much of that stuff that topples the ricks over." Hitting conceit off with a conceit !

Not that Glamorgan and the other counties are devoid of this fine art of the oblique. It was at Laleston that a farmer complained to me that his crop was not thriving—this was before the storms and before there was any talk of harvesting—" *Dôs dim lles o wynt Stalin !* " " Stalin's wind does no good." That, of course, was his way of referring to the east wind.

33

Had he been a poet he might have developed his quip by adding "*Ma' gwynt Stalin yn wara'r bér ar y cnwd!*" : "Stalin's wind is playing the bear with the crops!"

This reference to Russia at the moment is not pleasant, but it is at any rate a welcome change from the morbid reminder of a common Welsh phrase which describes the east wind as "*Gwynt traed y meirw*"—The wind of dead men's feet," a reference which only becomes clear when one remembers that graves lie west—east.

The storm and I visited Porthcawl too and seldom has one witnessed a more tempestuous sea, the snow-white spume making the rushing waters look blacker than ever.

Many have sought to register their reactions as they stand, and that with difficulty, watching the might of a storm-swept expanse of waters, but I hardly think that anyone has shouted finer words than those of the old Hebrew prophet :—

> The overflowing of the water passed by :
> The deep uttered its voice,
> And lifted up its hands on high.

10*th October*, 1950

Coal comes first

MAESTEG Railway Station at night : Maesteg Railway Station with snow along the platform : Maesteg Railway Station with its solitary, would-be traveller, anxiously waiting for the sound of a train that would take him home.

I didn't try to account for my movements to the porter-cum-ticket-collector.

It was only half-an-hour ago that he had accepted the half-ticket that had let me out of the station and he was now punching the other half to let me in, and possibly wondering what kind of business it was that could be transacted satisfactorily in half-an-hour.

Had I perhaps arrived too late for my engagement ? I was in no mood then to explain to him that I had come too early—by twenty-four hours.

But now that I am feeling warmer I don't mind confessing to the urge to lecture that had made me, for once, a man before my time, a whole day ahead of schedule.

"No," said the sympathetic official, as we both turned our heads in the direction of the oncoming sound, "that isn't your train. The coal train has to come before you."

34

And if I didn't know it before, I knew it then : the coal comes first to-day. He told me that the endless procession of trucks that presently rumbled along had all been filled at just two pits,— the Caerau and Coegnant—and that this was only one of many similar loads that passed through in the day.

And I thought of all the valleys in Wales and elsewhere with these ceaseless rivers of coal flowing through them.

How long will the supply last ? How is the gaping void left in the earth to be filled ?

They tell us that, at the moment, coal comes first but not yet have we accepted the corollary that the collier must come first.

Other work can be arduous, testing the human frame almost to breaking-point, or nerve-racking, or deadly monotonous, but it seems to me that few occupations can be more unnatural than cutting a grimy way through the rock and clay hundreds of yards below the surface, far from the light of day and the natural air with all the world on your back.

I know that no one will read this jeremiad with healthier scorn than the colliers themselves, who go singing to the pithead every morning.

They themselves never feel like this about it all, and what a good thing that is for the rest of us !

But I am not going back on what I said : if coal is to come first, the collier, too, is to be at the very head of the queue.

It *was* a cold night on the Maesteg Station : the would-be traveller, feeling miserably shy about his mistake, was eager to get home to hide his head, but even he quite agreed with the porter that the coal train had a prior claim to that pair of rails that left the station platform, white under the lamplight, for the black night, the factory, the home, and the sea.

17th October, 1950
A ruined castle

"NO, there isn't much to see," said the gentleman who allowed me to examine the ruined castle of Ogmore. But there was a great deal to feel. Indeed it was something more than the keen October wind that sent a cold shiver down my back as I crossed the little bridge and lingered among the dark walls.

Through one hole in the solid masonry one could follow the river almost down to the sea, and once or twice I almost thought that there was somebody peering over my shoulders, somebody watching anxiously, his breath on my neck.

No, there can't be much to see, especially if one's eyes are too lazy to rebuild broken masonry and re-roof the great halls, allowing the broken stems to flower again into stately pillars and arches.

I had meant to cross the stepping stones over which my ancestors at the castle had often crossed, but the river, helped by the autumn rains, had submerged half the stones and there was nothing for it but to find a bridge a little higher up.

Many a De Londres had crossed the green marshland that I now crossed on my way to Merthyr Mawr, a name that is older than the oldest Norman.

Then as now in autumn the green of the marsh was edged with the pale purple of withered thistle and the deep russet of the bracken, and then as now the great trees tried to hide Merthyr Mawr from the prying world.

The church door is always open not only to the devout peasantry but to people like myself who had come straight from the castle; and near the altar there was a part of a Celtic Cross, ancient enough to make me—by this time a genuine De Londres—feel that I was nothing but an upstart from over the water.

Unfortunately, I could not proceed further through the woods and into the gold of the sand-dunes for soldiers were at play there with weapons more lethal than bows and arrows; and I knew that a whistling bullet has no respect even for a genuine Norman knight !

28th November, 1950

Dead letters

WHICH would you say is the more futile, a man who has a message but no power of getting it across, or a man gifted with a dynamic appeal but with no worthwhile message ?

The question presented itself to me after a trifling incident that I find little pleasure in recording.

The secretary of a literary society had been kind enough to invite me to visit a district in West Wales, and as it was my father's birthplace I was eager to go.

However, there were difficulties in the way and I could not reply until I found out whether they could be surmounted. But to make sure that in the meantime I didn't forget the secretary's name and address I wrote them on a postcard straight away, meaning to pen an answer the next day.

The next day arrived and I couldn't find the postcard. How could I when I must have posted it with a bundle of other cards ?

Luckily I had kept the letter inviting me and I wrote apologising for the foolish blunder, only to find out just before posting time that I had on this occasion forgotten to fill in the name and address !

Both cards would have been of little value ; the second certainly bore a complete message, but it had no sense of direction ; the first was all direction and no message.

One had something to say, but it wouldn't have arrived. One arrived but it was dumb.

Have you sometimes been tempted to say after listening to an eloquent oration, " What a magnificent speaker if only he had something to say ! "

He had the invaluable gift of direct, personal appeal ; he had written the address on the card in a bold hand with many an artistic flourish, and it was definitely your own name and your own address. But when you turned the card over it was blank.

The other orator had his message. It was painstakingly sound and *painfully impersonal :* he didn't drive it home—he forgot to write the address and so it found its pathetic way to the dead-letter office.

5th December, 1950

Iolo Morgannwg

I WANT to say a word about Iolo Morgannwg. One accepts all the *facts* that wise and diligent scholarship has unearthed regarding this amazing man of the Vale of Glamorgan who has to be acknowledged as one of our great poets.

Until we hear of further discoveries that might possibly make us revise some of our verdicts, we acknowledge that he professed to have read and copied manuscripts that only existed in his too fertile brain.

But if we are to know the real man, there still remains the problem of the " moving why " he did it. Even in Penybont, on the very edge of the delectable Vale, there remains some confusion regarding this man of genius.

Said a Bridgend man to me—and he was one of the keenest men in the whole town—" That Iolo chap was a bit of a fraud, wasn't he ? " " A fraud ? " I asked, " a fraud in what way ? " " Didn't he come across some old poems by Dafydd ap Gwilym and palm them off as his own ? "

Of course that is exactly what he didn't do ; that brand of fraud would be intelligible though reprehensible—it holds no problem for us. What the scholars say is that Iolo composed poems so exactly like the glorious cywyddau of Ap Gwilym that everybody, including our greatest Welsh scholars, readily accepted his story that they were actually the master's ; indeed, the poems of the master at his very best.

Whatever the motive the amazing achievement remains and Professor Griffith John Williams himself, who has been on Iolo's tracks for a quarter of a century, would readily acknowledge what a marvellous thing it was that a stone-mason, completely self taught, could have so immersed himself in the fifteenth century that he not only caught the language and the literary idiom of that century, but also the poetic fancy of its immortal troubadour.

To confess that Iolo did all this does not then mean that we have found the real Iolo, especially when all are agreed that in his business and neighbourly transactions with his fellow-men no more honest man could be met anywhere.

Regarding the rites and ceremonies of *Yr Orsedd*, supposing it could be proved that no-one but Iolo ever saw the manuscripts, or are ever likely to see them, we must concede that " Old Iolo's " idea of what the Druidic rites were probably like is not to be easily dismissed.

Think of them, if you will, as of another *Cywydd* written in blue and green and white, whether actually inscribed on ancient vellum or not as authentic as this poet-historian could make them.

Wales need not give up reading " *Cywyddau yr Atodiad*," because the " D. ap G." signature is not really his, for the poems themselves are genuine " A. ap G." whoever wrote them.

As we have confessed, all this does not explain the vagaries of our enigmatic bard and antiquarian, but it does I hope suggest that Wales, rich in song but starved of colour, should not now turn its back upon a brilliantly thought-out spectacle that has for so long touched the nation's imagination.

And, of course, there is no longer any fear that it will do so. I myself believe that there is no need to introduce any new features ; but that again is a matter of personal feeling. I am satisfied that Iolo's symbolic pageant is almost complete.

A circle in an open field under an open sky where no-one is denied admission. An acknowledgment of God where no humble worshipper is denied.

A sheathed sword where peace is proclaimed. A gathering of men and women, the differing colour of whose robes only proclaims their interest in the different arts of their land.

Sons of Wales

ANOTHER Kalends of March has come and gone, the schools have been bright with Welsh-speaking daffodils and leeks, and banqueting halls and chapel vestries have rejoiced in menu cards whose startling Cymric names make every dish taste of Anwyl's dictionary.

Pulpits that all the year round have been reserved for Jewish patriarchs have opened their doors to a Welsh saint, and platforms have rung with the names of eminent sons and daughters of Wales.

Speaking of Wales's contribution to the arts, our orators often bemoan the fact that, while we have done something for music and for literature, we are a bankrupt nation as far as the visual arts are concerned. Indeed, I remember talking like that myself on one occasion, when I was delighted to be pulled up sharply by an impatient questioner—" Who gave Britain its greatest living artist ? "

And with the name of Augustus John reminding me of another John I am inclined to interrupt myself with a further query, " Who gave Britain its greatest living sculptor ? "

It is not so long ago that I saw the straight, spare figure of Sir William Goscombe John standing at the desk in the Welsh National Museum and chatting with the uniformed attendants as if he were one of them.

As indeed he was. No one has " attended " to the wants of our Museum with greater zeal and generosity. He has not only enriched it with the finest samples of his own skill but he has presented the nation with the works of many of the world's eminent sculptors and painters.

Goscombe John exhibited at the Royal Academy as far back as 1886, and for more than sixty years without a break his work has been shown there.

At how many St. David's Day celebrations was the name of Goscombe John mentioned ?

Lines in the sky

THE path I followed used to dwindle through the fields—and before I go further along that path you may want to thank me for this new-non-dictionary meaning of the word " dwindle." But it isn't really mine. I first heard it so used at Saundersfoot when an old lady told me that I needn't go round the high road to Tenby, for there was " a little path that dwindled right through the woods."

By to-day the field I mention has almost become a park and the path itself has broadened out almost beyond recognition ; its edges have been ruled into two straight lines and its surface has been firmly dealt with by the heavy-footed Mr. McAdam.

Along the edges at regular intervals I found two rows of tallish props, and at the far end two men were digging holes and fixing still more. They explained to me that the props were there to stand side by side with sapling trees, not yet planted, and I thought it was a good idea, for once the young tree started growing it would know exactly how to get about it, and if ever a wilful sapling thought of leaving the perpendicular there would be its silent mentor at hand to point out the error of its ways, just as my old schoolmaster's ruler placed beneath a crooked line of writing spoke censure with every one of its 12 inches. These men were simply placing their six-foot rulers on end before the trees started writing their leafy lines between the twin margins of earth and sky.

3rd April, 1951

The undying spirit

WITH Easter just behind us it would not be out of place to strike a note that is not often sounded in this column. Moreover, the simple incident I am about to chronicle seemed to me to have a certain Easter significance.

It was at Glyn Taf, and when the last rites had been observed, two young women who had lost their mother were perparing to re-enter the car and make for home.

They were deeply distressed but not too engulfed in their own grief to notice that an elderly relative who had come a long way was looking ill and faint, and when they learned that he had quite a time to wait for his bus, they felt that something had to be done. They were satisfied only when he agreed to come with them to their home.

When all was at last arranged, one of the sisters, again overcome by grief, turned to the minister—" I shall never see my mother again."

The minister answered quietly, " But I saw her now. It was your mother that I saw forgetting her own trouble, her heart going out to another's distress. It was good to see your mother again."

The breathing clay

I HAVE never claimed to possess second sight, but what happened certainly surprised me. Seeing something in the field, about the size of a small rabbit, I stood stock still and looked ; and it seemed to move.

When I approached it I found it to be nothing but a lump of clay. The apparent movement in such a case is not at all surprising and I have noticed it time and again.

Once you imagine that a thing is alive the next bit of imagining is almost inevitable. I expect it is merely a case of running your mental car in reverse. You have so often argued that a thing that moves must be alive that almost unconsciously, once you are convinced that there is life, you see or think you see movement.

No, that wasn't the surprising thing I have in mind. When I approached the lump of clay that had almost jumped to life at the breath of my imagination I saw another lump, and this time—there was no mistaking it—it was actually moving slowly, but surely, towards me and its twin brother lump.

As it waddled along, turning its tiny bear's head from side to side looking for what I don't know, I at last recognised brother hedgehog, but I cannot yet understand how or why I had seen it, as it were, fully two minutes before it had appeared.

As I watched its progress through the grass I couldn't help remembering one of the cuts in our school reader ; it was a picture of a horse clad in mail, or in some ceremonial garb perhaps, with just the hooves and fetlocks showing beneath its sweeping skirts.

Only that the busy, labouring gait of the poor fellow in the grass bore no resemblance to the proud prancing of my reader's steed.

As if to prove that its godfather had not mis-named him, the tiny " hog " moved on to the " hedge " and he didn't seem to mind it in the least that I went along with him. As a matter of fact I was beginning to feel that his studied unawareness of my presence was going a little too far.

Not to show abject fear of me was naturally a compliment that I appreciated, but, after all, I was many times his size, and he might have shown some sign of respect instead of carrying on as if I weren't there.

So, insisting on my human rights, I at last stamped my resentful foot near the brambles which he had now reached, and thinking he might as well please my vanity his glossy-coated liveliness became a prickly ball, as dead as the dead lump of clay that had started my story in the field.

A modern Elijah

MANY critics reject the story of Elijah and the ravens, but on different grounds. I was once telling the tale to a little, fellow who is to-day a Baptist minister and he, the young realist, immediately pounced on the improbability that a self-respecting prophet could have eaten stuff that had been lodged in a crow's mouth.

I wonder whether the Rev. Idris Morris is still of the same fastidious, epicurean mind ?

Another rejection involves a suggested textual emendation and one is reminded of a certain occasion when it was publicly put forward in the hearing of Silyn Evans, the vivid, inimitable minister of Aberdare.

A visiting preacher was holding forth and Silyn, sitting directly behind him in the pulpit, was encouraging him for all he was worth with many a high-pitched " Amen ! " These fervent ejaculations punctuated every other sentence almost, and the whole thing was possibly becoming an automatic performance.

Said the preacher : " Many commentators believe that the Hebrew word here translated ' ravens ' ought to have been another word very much like it, a word which means ' the Arabs,' " and before Silyn had time to grasp the miracle-destroying implication of this suggestion the explosive " Amen ! " had been released, but with the same breath came his withering *sotto voce* " Ach y fi ! "

This morning I was lucky enough to have a little coal, but there were no sticks. (It had been the other way about for some days.) And I was beginning to wonder whether old " Western Mails " and " Daily Heralds " would for once be persuaded to join hands and help me out, when I was amazed to find a pile of dried twigs ready to my hand in the grate.

This time there was no room for a child's objection, for the prophet was not expected to eat the twigs ; neither was there any call for textual tinkering for no Arab could ever have climbed to our high chimney pot.

Lest there should be any modernist sceptics among my readers I called in a reliable witness. Yes, there were at least 20 twigs, and with a 12-inch ruler I measured the three longest, to find that each extended many inches beyond the figure 12.

Of course one cannot know how in after years this may come to be written. Will it be like this ?

And the prophet dwelt in an house but the chamber thereof was nigher the roof than the ground thereof.

*And it came to pass at the breaking of day that the prophet perceived
that he had not wherewith to kindle a fire.*

*And the ravens rested on the roof as they built their nests for it
was the time of nests and the one said to the other.*

*" Lo, the old prophet this day sendeth no smoke to greet us, perchance
he lacketh fuel. Come let us divide with him."*

*And returning to the forest one brought a goodly twig and made
it to fall into the chimney ; and so did they all.*

*And the prophet beheld the kindling drop from heaven and
thereupon he kneeled, and kneeling lit a fire ; and lo, when
the ravens beheld the smoke ascending they rejoiced, making
a glad noise.*

If that be the chronicle of the future it will have departed from
the plain truth in at least one particular, for as a matter of fact the
prophet, feeling uneasy about a possible nest with young tenants,
turned on a switch and enjoyed the beaming " three cheers " of an
electric fire.

15th May, 1951

Men of Llangranog

LOOKED at from the beach at Llangranog, the observation
hut at the top of Dinas Lochtyn seems to be poised at a pro-
digious height. Or, if you persist in calling it a " pill-box," the
medicine chest on which it is placed is impossibly tall.

But though I am no mountaineer, even I was able to reach the
hut quite comfortably, for there is a zig-zagging road of a kind that
coaxes you up to within 50 yards of it. And once there the expanse
of land and sea that spreads out beneath you has to be seen to be
believed.

Some of us have for years been starved of this sense of spacious-
ness and like a boy at a party I feasted long and then stuffed my
pockets, preparing myself for the " cribbed, cabined and confined "
days that are to come.

And you will find the same sort of thing in the eyes of some
of the good men of Llangranog. One morning I hindered a
gardener at his work, taking it for granted that at 81 the most
zealous " man with a hoe " would not object to an occasional spell.

I wasn't long before finding that his merry eyes carried in their
depths the reflections of many distant seas and that he had once
known something more exciting than hoeing potato furrows.

" Another two months and I would have been 50 years at sea."
That meant, of course, that he had sailed for years when the winds
of heaven did duty for coal and oil and electricity—" and those
boats were much cleaner and more comfortable than the ones I
knew later."

And then back again to the present and to the foot-deep
furrows of earth, for at hilly Llangranog all gardens see each other
clearly all the time, and so in April and May, in a grand spirit
of emulation, every man who is not at sea is toiling in his garden.

When the whole countryside is gay with wild flowers, primroses,
cowslips, violets, bluebells, blackthorn and gorse, it is strange that
men and women still plant blooms in their plots.

Though I cannot boast of my mariner friend's 81 years, in my
whole life I have never known such a profusion of pleasing colours.

Late one evening I was one of a party of four at a cottage
fireplace. I am not sure what had brought the other three together
but I couldn't forget that the morrow was the last day for posting
literary compositions for the Llanrwst National Eisteddfod; and
these men were all seasoned eisteddfodwyr.

But they were canny Cardis, too, and not one of them was
prepared to disclose to the others what he was about to send in.

Indeed they all volunteered and all pretended to accept the
innocent fiction that they had written nothing for Llanrwst ; but
as I looked round, and as I knew who was later to join them, I
realised that here under one roof you had a bunch of the most
accomplished masters of the Welsh strict metres ; two of them
had taken the National *englyn* prize, one at Caerphilly, the other
at Dolgellau, while the other two had given them a hard run.

It was a liberal education to hear so much sound sense wrapped
up in the homely banter and argument of some of Llangranog's
unassuming men of letters.

22nd May, 1951

Festival time

I EXPECT that over the holiday you, too, celebrated the Festival
in some field or other. At our own merry-making when I chose
my seat under the trees I had no idea that the organisers had hung
a leather-lunged loudspeaker in the leafy branches right above my
innocent head. But I soon knew it was there !

When our fine local band played at the far end of the field, at
a safe distance from the microphone, it sounded as a band should
sound ; but when the " mike " got hold of it you can imagine
the effect.

And when a succession of records kept on going round and round I couldn't help feeling sorry for the poor athletes, on their marks, crouching tensely there, while the leaves above them shook with mighty, crooning sighs and thunderous whispers.

Those unbroken records at the microphone were perhaps largely responsible for some unbroken records at the tape.

But please do not imagine that we didn't have a good time in these well-organised festivities. The only misfortune was that two hyper-sensitive ears found themselves too near Stentor's lips of brass.

And how were the organisers to know that a thrush was going to invite himself as an additional guest artiste ?

Without the formality of an audition, or letting Mansel Thomas know anything about it, he was actually at the microphone, but I feel sure that he had no idea there was this amplifier to convert his liquid song into a series of piercing screams.

As I moved away I realised that the best things in the world can become the worst by the simple process of making them bigger than themselves.

There was some excuse for the thrush, but I do not know what to say about the rest of us who are not prepared to sing or even to speak until we know that there is a loudspeaker somewhere at the end of the wire.

Said a friend to an artist who had just finished painting a portrait, " But wasn't it a commission for a life-size picture ? That is surely bigger than life."

" Yes," answered the artist, who was a philosopher as well as a painter, " I have painted him the size he thinks he is."

And most of our self-portraits, dared we show them to the public, are like that. Wisely enough, the man who wants to keep his reputation for humility only exhibits them in his private gallery open only to himself, his wife, and his dear mother. He can't trust his own children even into this special gallery, for they may have colder and more critical eyes, and may feel that both picture and frame are rather too big.

5th June, 1951

The dandelion clock

NEAR the bus stop there is a field corner where trees grow, and you will look more than once at these trees because the shadows they cast are masses of bluebells. In the field a little girl with tense eyes and puffed out cheeks is trying to force a feathery ball of dandelion seeds to tell her the time.

Though hundreds of children up and down the country are daily carrying out the same ritual, what makes this particular instance rather noteworthy is that in the field exactly opposite the biggest and most modern clock factory in Wales is staring at her.

Not for a moment do you and I question the quality and reliability of the factory clocks, but it is possible that many of us would rather like to set our watches once again by the numbered puffs of childhood. Some of us, perhaps, have insisted on doing so for a lifetime and that is why we have, in more senses than one, " missed the bus."

However, I caught this morning's without any difficulty and I found a good seat near the front, a good seat with two definite drawbacks ; it was on the side away from the sun and it was a viewless seat, for the driver had pulled down the blind behind him.

As yet the conductor had not approached me and so I felt free to change over to the other side (it is rather mean to move somewhere else after the conductor's eye has fixed you in your corner, for, as you must have noticed, the man with the tickets only knows you by your corner ; he takes no interest in the fact that you are bald-headed or round-shouldered, or mackintoshed or what not).

I had now an uninterrupted view of the valley through which we twisted, for I could never describe the woman's hat as an interruption ; furthermore, the bunched, deep-toned lilacs that she carried were soon as much mine as hers, for, sitting directly behind her, most of the rich colour and fragrance came back to me, the only thing she kept to herself being the joy of carrying them.

The bus could hardly claim to be following the exact course of the Tawe although both ran through the same valley along Trebanos, Clydach, Treforus, Plasmarl, Glandwr, on to the " Aber " of both river and bus end.

We took different routes occasionally and indeed at certain points we lost sight of each other completely.

Much more consistent in its companionship was the canal which like a dependable spirit-level showed us precisely when our road took us up-hill or down-dale. As we got nearer Swansea, because we had got so interested in each other, I was grieved to notice that its clear water was now a stream of thick yellow ochre.

At Clydach most of the passengers took a quick glance skywards and then turned to look away just as quickly, for near the sky-scraping top of one of the highest stacks at " The Monds " three or four steeplejacks were erecting a tubular scaffolding.

They looked like ants crawling over a pigmy meccano set. I threw a coat over my knees because they had become suddenly limp and cold and shivery.

Boyhood road

SOME of us have arrived at the age when the predominant urge is to recapture rather than to capture. When one morning I set out on a country road, on the border of Carmarthen and Pembroke, I didn't exactly know what I wanted to recapture, but the pining desire was certainly there.

I had known this road, every inch of it, when I was a boy, but though I realised how foolish it was to dream of knowing again the vitality of boyhood I couldn't help hoping that something of the past was still left in the air.

I had to pass the village shop—if you can call four cottages a village, and a few shelves a shop—which that day boasted but two sorts of sweets, and though I came away with samples of both in my pockets neither sort would take me back where I would be. I had hoped that there might have been a bottle of white " extra-strongs " or pear-shaped " lemon drops."

Even with this initial setback I did not lose heart ; I still realised that boyhood, if it was to come back at all, would return by way of my mouth, and so I hopefully scanned the hedges.

The quiet but unambiguous taste of whinberries did their best for me as I remembered the high hedge near Moriah on a Sunday morning. In that long ago we were anxious not to empurple our lips as we never felt satisfied that picking the Sunday berries bore the imprimatur of the papal decrees from our " Big Seat."

With the help of my umbrella crook I pulled down some over-hanging hazel branches and, though the nuts were far from ripe, the taste, something between that of milk and raw mushrooms, was certainly evocative, and before long the boy that I was looking for seemed to be walking at my side.

It was such a pity that the Ffynnon Wen motor-car, modernity incarnate, came round the corner at that very moment. Dilwyn at the wheel beamed at me as he careered by, blissfully ignorant of the fact that he had driven the little fellow who was with me into the ditch.

'Take a seat, please'

"**P**LEASE take a seat." Just a well-mannered conventional phrase that can be heard in all sorts of places on all sorts of occasions. But no, not quite.

Until the late Daniel Hopkin uttered it, and that almost as a matter of course, it had seldom, if ever, been heard in a magistrate's court, especially when the person invited to take a seat was a prisoner in the dock.

If Daniel Hopkin had had his way the dock, separating a man from his fellows, would have had to go the way of all unpleasant mediaeval judicial relics.

As yet I myself have not been asked to stand in that terrifying pulpit, whose only Bible is a never-opened one, to be held up in the hand while, sexton-like, you repeat the chanted formula of " the truth, the whole truth, and nothing but the truth."

It is bad enough to stand there even as a witness when the whole stiff-backed proceeding, with the minatory stare of all concerned, contrives to make you feel guilty of some crime or other, if you could only remember what it was !

Daniel Hopkin succeeded in making a man feel that however guilty he was he wasn't a hunted creature cornered at last, with all the polished buttons of England ranged against him and every awe-inspiring wig curling with vengeance.

In a sense every man charged in his court was asked to take part in the deliberations ; he was asked to " take a seat " ; he was invited to see what a difficult position he was creating for his fellows by his anti-social activities. And though the remedy suggested had often to be of a drastic nature many of the men who took the medicine, if one is to judge by certain funeral tributes, recognised that it was meant as a remedy.

I fear that those called upon to " administer justice " do not receive the sympathy they deserve at the hands of the nation, for there can be no more uncongenial task than that of sitting in judgment right through the year, day in and day out. From the village constable to the judge on his bench, all have to keep an eye on the offender, and that is no pleasant duty.

It is fortunate that judges, lawyers, and policemen have other interests strong enough to take mind and soul outside the court-room. I once had occasion to attend an assize case at Cardiff, when I was particularly interested in the keen, business-like pleading of one of the barristers.

When the case was over I was surprised to receive a message from him : Could I step up to have a word ? As I went I wondered whether perhaps he wanted to give me some information regarding the man whom he had successfully defended, for he knew that I was interested in him. You can judge of my surprise to find that all he wanted to consult me about was the translation of a certain Welsh hymn !

One has to thank our courts for many a sample of good pleading and ready retort. It was at Cardiff that I heard Lord Carson, whose heavy sheath of a jaw housed a rapier tongue.

It was at Dolgelley that I heard Ellis Griffith who in some respects was his Welsh counterpart. It was a sheep-stealing case, and in the eyes of a pastor " sheep-stealing " is no venial crime !

The son of Anglesey, with thunder in his face, was finding fault with a witness who slouched in the witness-box. " Take your hands out of your pockets ! " The poor fellow readily obeyed, but in the meantime the judge was suavely pointing out to Ellis Griffith that a witness was perfectly entitled to do what he liked with his hands.

" Very well, you can put them back in your pockets ! " If it was pathetic to see the hands withdrawn it was even more so to see them clumsily replaced.

Many stories will be related of Daniel Hopkin, but I shall prefer to remember him as the " Please take a seat Magistrate."

18th September, 1951

Bench in the brambles

THOUGH there are many comfortable seats ranged round the field, the only one where I could count on solitude was the narrow bench in the brambles at the far end of the cricket pitch ; and even there, on the other side of the hedge there was a postman off duty picking blackberries, and every so often his companionable dog would come nosing round to see what I was up to.

Had an artist been sitting where I sat the glaringly white screen in front would have answered a good purpose for, were he tempted to treat those clouds as pure white, the screen would have shouted at him how wrong he was.

The cricket season is over and I cannot pretend that the empty pitch is as full of shades as Lord's was to Francis Thompson when he sang :

And a ghostly batsman plays to the bowling of a ghost,
And I look through my tears on a soundless clapping host
  As the run-stealers flicker to and fro,
  To and fro—
O my Hornby and my Barlow long ago.

49

This field is not Lord's and though it has known many a fine match it hasn't as yet been rolled long enough to grow ghosts.

Beyond the sight-screen the newly-painted goal-posts are up, their white length gay with splashes of blue to encourage the local XV.

The paint is new, and so are the posts. Too new to please me. I asked the groundsman whether it was quite safe to use these tubular steel posts : what if a dashing player diving for a try collided with one of them ?

" Oh, well," he answered, " timber is pretty solid, too," referring of course, not to the player's head but to the old posts, that had grown in a forest and not in a steelworks.

I cannot say whether the groundsman I spoke to is a "full-time " man or not, but he certainly has interests outside both cricket and football, and in his enthusiasm he has persuaded many of us that there is hardly anything in the world more beautiful than a Labrador retriever.

His own black beauty sports a very dignified name on the show catalogues but though he retrieves so many cups and cards, when he romps about the home fields he doesn't mind our calling him " Ben."

Just beyond the farther goal-posts is another playing-pitch, the circle of stones where the Archdruid and his merry men more than once played their spectacular games.

You will see many similar Circles in different parts of Wales, but this particular one is unique. In no other place was a Proclamation Ceremony held which was not followed in a year and a day by the Eisteddfod itself, and these grey stones are greyer than all the rest because of their war years of frustration and disappointment.

But the Bridgend National was worth waiting for ; that is what I try to tell the stones when they look at me with such tragic, woe-begone countenances.

Then above the trees the gleaming spire of Nolton. It is more than stone. The joy of physical exercise and the friendly pitting of team against team ; the proclaiming of art and poetry and song, and then the upward pointing of a white finger.

In an age to come people may ask what purpose these steeples dotted all over the country could have served. Let me answer. They were our forefathers' pylons whose unseen wires transmitted unseen power.

Collared!

THIS is the tale of a butterfly wing; not the fluttering, multi-coloured, gossamer-light variety, but the white, solidly-starched band that holds a man by the neck, little heeding whether it chokes him or not.

I believe I am right technically in so naming this particular brand of collar, though I learn that the Rhondda outfitters have been long accustomed to another designation.

The young collier who will be singing on Saturday night at the Judge's-hall, when he orders this style, uses a term that might well be mistaken for a fervent evangelical appeal, a term which I refrain from pinning on paper, lest it should gain wider currency.

This collar entered my life when one evening two easy spoken but tenacious men called upon me to insist that I should wear one. And they had come all the way from Llandilo.

Didn't I adjudicate at the Aberafan Eisteddfod when Amanwy almost carried off the Crown? Wasn't I chosen to read out the summarised adjudication in the pavilion?

They were making a Welsh Festival of Britain film, and Amanwy, or " David " as they chose to call him, was their typical Welshman for the picture. I agreed to come to Ammanford to re-enact the Eisteddfod scene to the best of my ability; indeed, I was almost enthusiastic—until the butterfly landed on the flowers.

Though I pleaded that I didn't mind a dog-collar or the flat-lying variety or no collar at all, it was no good.

" Don't you see," they argued, " we haven't a picture of that long-ago affair in Aberafan so we have taken and shall use the Caerphilly ceremony.

The cinema audience will be shown the actual photograph of an adjudication being delivered at Caerphilly, but in that second's glimpse they won't be able to make out the actual figures on the distant stage ; so we shall give them a close-up of the adjudicator— and by that time it will be you, and you in Aberafan.

" But I'm sure that I never sported a butterfly in Aberafan ! "
" Perhaps you didn't, but the fellow in Caerphilly did : and it would never do to allow an actor to change his collar on the journey from the far view to a close up ! "

And thus it was that the improvised studio at Ammanford found me with a strange new collar about my self-conscious ears. But that was only the beginning.

The lights had to be so arranged that the shadows fell on my face exactly as they fell on his face on the distant stage.

And never was there such shifting about of high-powered lamps while I, patience on a chair, stood stock-still under the blinding bombardment.

Worse was to follow. " David " was to hear the beginning of the adjudication from outside the pavilion, so right round the room the heavy amplifiers had to be ranged and tested one by one, and so you can imagine how often my little piece had to be trotted out while the trusty studs holding on to their new collar almost gave way at the reiterated swelling passages.

But, of course, it was David's picture—my wing collar was beginning to imagine that the film was his !—and the whole battery had now to concentrate on Amanwy's face as he listened to the fateful adjudication, and what a fine face it is !

I believe that the old hands marvelled at its expressiveness ; not the exaggerated emotion-registering of the cinema, but the real thing, the emotion revealing itself in its very struggle for concealment.

But in the final " shooting " there was almost a final calamity. I had been wearing glasses and the man on the stage had none, and I was told peremptorily that mine would have to come off.

But on this even I was for once adamant. It was useless for them to suggest that if I couldn't read the short summary I could learn it : I who have never been able to learn two consecutive sentences.

It was a proper hold-up, and I fear that my butterfly-wing sacrifice would have been all in vain but for the keen eyes, or keen wit, of a woman secretary who had been peering at the tiny square-inch picture on the film.

" It is quite all right," she exclaimed, " if you look carefully you will see that he has his glasses in his hand."

So that was that. If he carried glasses—and I had only my new found friend's word for it—what was more natural than that he should put them on for his close-up ?

And what became of the historic collar ? That is a story whose sequel I am not sure of. All I know is that at 12 o'clock that night it was presented, with due ceremony, to a young Methodist minister who was soon to preach his first sermon in the Sasiwn.

I afterwards heard glowing reports of that memorable service, but I hadn't the courage to ask my informant whether the young preacher was wearing a butterfly wing.

The 'high-ups'

I HAD never before seen the woman who leaned on her long brush-handle outside her door, but the weather is always a safe introduction card, and she didn't resent my conversational approach—" Do you think we are going to have rain ? "

" I shouldn't be surprised," she answered ; " I see that the cockerel has gone to look for it."

Before answering she had cast her eyes aloft for a second ; and I ought to have explained that we were standing right under the ancient church tower.

Her " cockerel," of course, was the golden bird caged between four capital letters, W. and E., N. and S., and when I, too, looked up I saw that he was peering lightheartedly enough between the S. and the W. looking for rain, though from his high perch he must have seen the many impatient stooks still ungathered.

It is no wonder that " the cockerel " takes himself so seriously when he finds all eyes turned up reverently to him ; and by this time he fondly imagines that it is he who turns the winds of heaven round.

We do not unduly blame him for he is only adopting the logic of so many other full-breasted high-ups that we have known.

Autumn colours

A BLIND man, especially a blind man endowed with the optimistic temperament and intellectual quality of Puleston Jones, may succeed, despite his handicap, in reaping almost full enjoyment from life, but as I walked in the country yesterday I realised that there is one whole world denied him, the world of colour.

What is there that can compensate the heart that has no share in autumn's prodigality ? What a variety of tints ! You may name gold, copper, orange, russet, and red, but then each colour has its own individual scale of tones and semi-tones, and you would be hard put to label each.

Two months ago the leaves in their prime crowded together under the general green flag ; it was a kind of mass vitality where individuality was not marked.

When those leaves were younger it was easier to tell the one from the other though the tints only ranged through yellows and greens with suggestions of violet ; and now again, when old age is come upon them, they become more and more themselves ; before finally losing grip and letting go, for one brief moment, they insist on their own personality and refuse to be merged in the mass.

Let me pick them out over there round Broadlands, one by one now. Though I do not know their names I salute their individual personalities. We old people at the last have a right to be ourselves.

Shattering my rather solemn meditation or, rather, giving it a fresh turn, a new tree stood up, straighter than the straightest pine, blue against all the yellows behind it.

It had its roots in the chimney stack of a cottage, and so it couldn't be truly counted among the real trees of the wood.

The blue smoke is but the ghost of a tree that has gone ; all its colours merged in the blue that is now seeking the purer blue of heaven.

20th November, 1951

At second-hand

HOW easy it is to fall into error when chronicling a conversation, especially when one conversed with little thought of subsequent reporting, and when days have elapsed between the event and its actual report.

But sometimes things can go wrong even when the speaking and the repeating are almost simultaneous.

At a stile in Newbridge fields I met a number of boys ; two or three had already crossed before they noticed that I was there, and I greeted them with my " Good morning, boys."

The other two or three stood back for me to cross and then they got over ; and when they caught up with their friends I heard one of them ask : " What did he tell you ? "

I smiled when I heard the reply ; in substance perhaps correct enough, but certainly not *ipsissima verba :* " Oh, he only said ' 'Ullo, kids ! ' "

A missing lecturer

IT was pitch dark when I woke up, and my watch, which tells the time in the dark, said that it was five o'clock. But no sooner had I turned round to go to sleep again than I half remembered something.

No, surely not! But to make sure I switched on the electric light, and got up to fumble for my notecase; and in the diary I found what I had vainly hoped wasn't there.

There it was staring me in the face. "November 23, Friday. Laleston Primary School, 7.30."

And it was now November 24, Saturday, and I had been to no Laleston Primary School on the previous night; I had completely forgotten the promised lecture.

Any idea of sleeping on had now vanished. I had no excuse to offer. If any had come to hear me, they must have come through the pelting rain, for you may remember what November 23, Friday, was like.

Between five and seven I had ample time to relish my misery to the full. The only consolation—although it wouldn't help matters between me and Laleston—was remembering how very seldom, in a longish life of public work, I had failed to remember an engagement.

One lapse stood out. I had been particularly glad of an invitation to a St. David's Day function at the Hengoed Girls' School, but St. David and I got slightly mixed over the actual date and I wasn't there to meet him.

Speaking of engagements, it is easier to forget a wedding than a funeral.

In the nature of things the time between the notice and the funeral is but a matter of days, whereas three weeks or three months even may elapse between the evening when two young people come to see you—you having to help them out almost to the point of telling them what they want to tell you—and the morning of the marriage.

But it was only on two occasions that my memory played me a trick over a wedding. On the first, hot-foot messengers had to rush from the church—a nearby church, fortunately, to fetch me. With the second, it was only the intervention of a special Providence which saved me, and that at the very last moment.

I was actually making for the station to catch the morning train, my road taking me past our church.

As I was about to pass it I was surprised to see the front doors open, and there in the porch was the chapel-keeper. " They have just arrived now," she whispered.

I walked unhurriedly up the aisle, and in two seconds the ceremony was under way, the young people, I feel sure, praising me for having arranged things so perfectly. What if they knew how near they had been to catastrophe !

For most ministers a wedding day is a delight (I refer of course to other people's weddings, though—with another saving " of course "—one doesn't of necessity preclude one's own). The only drawback is the questionnaire levelled at one on arrival back home.

I have never been an authority on the exact colour and material favoured by bride and bridesmaids, and I have before now stumbled badly when, eager to show off my easy familiarity with such things as style, I have referred to a " three-piece," not realising that such a thing belongs more to the world of suites than to that of suits.

In order to prove how knowledgeable I am in such matters I even venture to refer to the " accessories," ending the first syllable with the double " s " demanded by up to date dressmakers.

Not that I fail to be impressed, and sometimes overwhelmingly so, by the beauty of certain " creations," but on seeking under subsequent cross-examination to recall the vision splendid I am never sure whether it was pink or purple, blue or white that has bowled me over.

Some time ago, at a bus stop, a woman spoke to me, and she was rather taken aback that I didn't immediately recollect who she was. " But you married me ! " she exclaimed.

I tried to excuse myself when she explained that it was some years ago. " But don't you remember ? I was wearing mauve."

" Oh, mauve ! " I exclaimed pseudo-ecstatically as a kindly Western Welsh great whale arrived and swallowed me up.

Echoes

ROUND about Christmas and the closing year it was good to find one's feet again on an old, familiar road. As I approached a well-remembered railway arch a Valley train was just rattling over it in fine style, and though I had every confidence in the bridge, I didn't venture under it until the last coach was safely across. The remarkable thing is, not one's momentary hesitation, but one's abiding, matter-of-course confidence in the bridges that have to shoulder such heavy loads.

Of course, I, too, have heard of " the principle of the arch," but I have not ceased to be amazed that a railway train can be held up by a mere principle, by a mathematician's dream.

When I got right under the arch anybody who might have been watching would have been surprised to see a more or less normally sane many indulging in a sudden round of vigorous hand-clapping.

It wasn't that I was applauding the genius who first thought of inviting a train to trust itself to a mathematical principle. I was merely asking the old archway whether it still afforded hospitality to the echo that once used to haunt its dark roof.

It was there still. My first clap came back, indeed, it came back with interest, reverberating. And as I kept it up for some time, between the echo's busy hands and mine, the reporter's bracketed " loud applause " would be an inevitable description of the tumult that ensued.

The scientists are able to speak with authority of " the principle of the arch," but they are still fumbling in the dark after the secret of the echo.

Even Christopher Wren, who arched the dome of St. Paul's, was baffled by the elusive laws of echoland, and even to-day, when so many acousticians have been hard at work throughout the years, the man in St. Paul's pulpit has to compete with a score of gay sextons who mock and mimic his syllables ; and when the choir sings, another mystic unsurpliced crowd joins in with its every note a fraction of a second too late.

Most of us who try to speak in public have known this irritating fooling of a mocking echo, but sometimes when Echo and all its vassals have been *completely* banished from a room the experience can be even more disconcerting.

I have seen a company of radio actors enter a room in the best of spirits, but once inside the draped and padded studio, where they find their voices falling dead on the cushioned air, a strange melancholy depresses their spirit to a sepulchural zero ; and perhaps they are there for a humorous turn !

Dante describes a group of unfortunates in the other world who had no shadows and I almost think that a voice that casts no shadow at all would also suffer the pangs of purgatory.

Ieuan Gwynedd

WHEN I lived in Cardiff I was always proud to show visitors the house in the heart of the city where Ieuan Gwynedd, poet and prophet, had spent the closing years of his short but strenuous life.

Often had I heard talk of placing a plaque on that historic building, but, as far as I know, nothing came of it. And now it is almost too late.

The house, where Ieuan Gwynedd breathed his last, just 100 years to this very month, still stands ; but it is now on the very edge of the new roadway which has been created for the traffic that races through the city.

When the great new road was mooted some of us were crazy enough to think that the authorities would honour themselves and the young prophet by linking Ieuan's name with it. But it was not to be.

With splendid pomp and ceremony the road was at last officially opened and by to-day we have all driven our cars over the wide macadam or tramped the broad pavements of " Churchill Way." But, name or no name, one yet hopes that Cardiff will not forget that a young man died just here, having given all the 31 years of his life to Wales.

To the end, despite bodily pain and the shattering of many a brave dream, he continued to write, indeed, within a day or two of his death he was busily composing a new poem.

Was he pouring his personal grief and disappointment into these last lines ? The poem was at last finished. And the title ? " The Colliers' Sufferings." To the last it was not of himself he thought, but the poor, the maligned, the down-trodden ; and especially the miners for whom he had preached and pleaded at Tredegar.

A few years ago I was preaching at Ieuan's old church at Saron, Tredegar. In the afternoon a great Labour open-air session was to be held at the Waun Pond on the heights between Tredegar and Ebbw Vale, and with the crowd, I, too, climbed through Sirhowy.

It was a moving spectacle. They came in endless processions, all converging to the banks of the pond, where a platform had been erected, high enough and solid enough to hold the weight of Aneurin Bevan's eloquent message.

I couldn't help realising that these miners were the grand-sons and great-grandsons of the very men for whom Ieuan Gwynedd had given himself; neither could I help asking myself whether one in ten of those crowding around me had ever heard of his name.

However, it is good to remember that the young preacher had known nothing but kindness during his years in Monmouthshire, and how sorry he was to announce his resignation from their pulpit.

Too broken for further public work, he still wielded a mighty pen. When a Royal Commission on Education in Wales published its findings in those notorious Blue Books, all Welsh leaders felt that if such totally ill-informed and unjust conclusions were allowed to go unchallenged it would be tantamount to confessing that Wales, and especially the women of Wales, knew little of education and less of morality.

The heroic invalid of Tredegar, realising that mere fulminating would be useless, set about the colossal task of gathering unassailable evidence from many sources, and with statistics marshalled into fighting battalions he more than held his ground.

Who, then, was this young man who wrote such incisive English that he was appointed editor of the Cardiff " Principality " and of the London " Standard of Freedom " ?

It is hard to believe that a very few years previously he had lived in a remote glen in Merioneth, a monoglot peasant lad with nothing in the world but his own sterling character and the inspiration of a God-fearing home.

Emlyn Williams a few years ago had to invent a romance for his " Last Days of Dolwyn," placing it in the village of Rhydymain, without realising, perhaps, that in the very village, ready to his cunning hand, was one of the most romantic stories that Wales has ever known ; the story of Evan Jones, Ifan Ty-croes, learning to read his mother's " red Bible," speaking on temperance at a Dolgelley fair, struggling to enter Brecon College.

The house where he was born is to-day nothing but a sorry heap of black-grey stones and rubble, but on one of my periodic visits I was determined to find it and I was proud to carry away one tiny stone.

That sacred stone stands for Bryn Tynoriad and for Ieuan Gwynedd ; a bit of Meirionydd granite that is a challenge to any easy-going compromise or soft self-indulgence.

Friend and counsellor

" A GOOD man " ; that is a phrase that you must have heard time and again during the last few days. And it is a completely satisfactory phrase, for " good " does not carry with it any half-hidden suspicion of unpleasantness.

In the long ago of plenty it was a common sight to see a would-be customer at a market stall placing a morsel of butter to her lips, and then half-closing her eyes to get its full flavour. She takes her time. Is there just a suggestion of a " tail " of bitterness ? I didn't blame her for her critical acumen then and I do not blame her now.

You taste a word like " justice " ; a rich, golden, full-flavoured word ; but you can't turn it over long on the tip of your tongue without realising, or at least imagining, that there is a something about it that you don't care for.

You are told that the man is " absolutely just," and though you don't know him you immediately begin to wonder whether he isn't perhaps a little stern and censorious.

" There goes a very pious fellow ! " Piety is surely one of the noblest attributes of all, but this again, like " justice " has suffered because it has long been used without due care ; so that when you hear of a singularly " pious " man you may not be too eager to meet him.

There is no such hidden suggestion of bitterness in the word " good," and when you have said " he was a good man," he who hears you knows exactly what you mean.

" Good," moreover, owes no allegiance to any particular class or status. Unfortunately, the word " gentleman " has suffered a little in that way :

> *Defamed by every charlatan*
> *And soiled with all ignoble use.*

The common Welsh term for " gentleman " is gŵr bonheddig, and "bôn" means " stock," implying, I should imagine, that gentlemanliness to a Welshman is largely a matter of good breeding ; of branching from an ancient stock.

But in one of the Mabinogion tales I am glad to notice that a term is used which exactly corresponds to the " gentle " in " gentleman." When Teyrnion came across the foundling baby and noticed how he was clad he immediately realised that he was the son of " dynion mwyn," of " gentle folk."

Among those who have tried to rescue the " gentleman " from unworthy associations was Cardinal Newman and his words are worth remembering :

" He has his eyes on all his company ; he is tender towards the bashful, gentle towards the distant, and merciful towards the absurd. He guards against unreasonable allusions, or topics which may irritate ; he is seldom prominent in conversations, and never wearisome. He makes light of favours when he does them, and seems to be receiving when he confers them. He has no ears for slander, is scrupulous in imputing motives to those who interfere with him and interprets everything for the best. He is never mean or little in his disputes, never takes unfair advantage, never mistakes personalities or sharp sayings for arguments, or insinuates evil which he dare not say out."

Much will be spoken and written of the good man and gentleman that we have in mind, but we hardly think that many will improve on Stanley Baldwin's words when he sorrowed over the death of George V. And as the words are recalled does one not feel how fittingly they can be applied to the passing of the Sixth George ?

" It is less than a month ago that the voice now silent was heard round the world, a King addressing his subjects, a father seated with his family, speaking to his people, members of his wider family, words of wisdom, courage and deep human sympathy. And it is as members of a family that we are mourning him to-day. There must be millions who feel, as I do, that a wise and loving friend and counsellor has been taken from us, and for long the world will seem a poorer and a colder place. The tones of that well-known voice are echoing in our ears to-day as our thoughts turn to the widowed Queen and to the bereaved family."

28th February, 1952

Alas! What boots it ?

SINE QUA NON, " without which nothing," or so one would think ; but recently a Monmouthshire Valley football XV arrived at their rival club's dressing-room complete, but for their football boots !

I had reason to remember them as I thought of one whose well-documented " qualifications " for a job included very many extra accomplishments, but as he was expected to kick a particular ball about, it was a pity that he had no boots in his bag.

An old warrior, who perhaps knew more about football than about chapels, was trying to tell me that the ministers attending a local conference were supposed to leave their bags and their overcoats at a certain vestry ; and I knew exactly what he meant when, without seeking to be facetious, he said : " That is where the parsons go *to strip*."

One trusts the ministers, too, had remembered their football boots, for they have a tough game ahead of them these days, and it is to be hoped that they know the *sine qua non* of this vital conflict.

In the hard cement of a pathway leading to a front-door in our street I notice that a little fellow wearing no kind of boot has left footprints which no amount of scrubbing can now remove.

The dog, of course, must have scampered over the path when the cement was still wet, and thinking back I can now recall the very night when he so immortalised that brief chapter of his career.

The man had finished the job and at nightfall the owner of the house saw to it that the little gate was firmly shut ; indeed, several pieces of wire were tightly wound around the iron catch.

You will understand his concern when I tell you that it was then the pre-Christmas week when hordes of children would not let us forget that there was once a good king called Wenceslas ; these minstrels, unlike their " Herald Angels," boasted no wings, and it was from their boots that the wet path had to be so zealously guarded.

That dog, whoever he was, had no hand or paw in the making of this beautifully smooth pathway, but like many another honour-seeker he insisted on leaving his own trade mark upon it.

4th March, 1952

Memory

I BEGIN with a quotation :
> *Drive slowly, wisely choose,*
> *From drink forbear ;*
> *. . . . . . shake the tree,*
> *Down falls the pear.*

How many readers can name the author of these lines ? Were it a matter of mere guessing one would begin like the experienced quiz addict by narrowing the field of possible authors, asserting that the poet evidently belongs to the ultra-modern school.

Is it Joyce or Auden? The style rather rules out Dylan Thomas. While old-fashioned literary folk might jib at the apparent inconsequence of the staccato adjurations, any youthful critic who is well-up in this new writing could tell us how crystal clear it all is.

Isn't it merely a vivid tale of a soul-excursion where youth is cramped by frustrating old-age, with its accent on speed limits, stodgy deliberation, and abstinence?

Then, after the eloquent series of dots, we get·a glimpse of youth asserting itself and allowing its rejuvenated Old Adam to shake the life out of the orchard's pride. (Note the inspired, frenzied *joie de vivre* that turned the traditional apple-tree into a pear-tree.)

If you dared to ask your literary mentor how he explained that longish line of dots—did they represent a mental hiatus of some kind?—he would assure you that they, too, are charged with vital symbolism, pointing out that many a poet has made his name simply by writing it on the dotted line.

Which is, of course, all nonsense. You knew from the beginning, especially those of you who were brought up on Low's English Grammar, that the jingle is nothing but an aid to help you remember a list of " strong " verbs—drive, choose, bear, shake, fall—and the dots really represent my own lapse of memory ; for there are memories that can even forget a mnemonic !

At Eilir's centenary meeting last week, though much was said of his extraordinary gifts as cleric and journalist, I don't recollect that anyone referred to his amazing memory.

One solitary instance will prove how extraordinary it was. He had written an awdl of over a thousand lines for a Cardigan Town eisteddfod, and when his friends at Llandyssul heard that he had won the chair, nothing would do but that they should hear him read his poem, and a meeting was convened in the Long Room of the local inn—a fitting place for such a lengthy composition.

Eilir, who was then the village schoolmaster, duly arrived and though he had not kept a copy of the poem he experienced no difficulty in reciting the 1,100 lines of cynghanedd.

It took him over two hours, which speaks well not only of the reciter's tenacious memory but of the Long Roomers' interest in poetry. True, it was the day of long poems.

Ieuan Gwynedd's best-known poem is a little matter of 3,000 lines, while Dafydd Ionawr's " Ode to the Trinity " is 13,000 lines long.

It is perhaps largely due to my own defect in this direction that I note with a certain degree of envy any instance of outstanding prowess in the realm of memory.

Those who have attended recent National Eisteddfodau have marvelled not only at the literary and oratorical merits of Professor T. H. Parry-Williams's detailed adjudications, but at the sheer power that, without the help of a note, marshals easily the names of poets and the contents of each work, with extensive quotations.

The Rev. William Morris, Cynan and Gwenallt from among modern adjudicators, and Iolo Caernarfon from an earlier generation, are others who have often displayed this amazing gift.

When I once mentioned this matter to Professor Parry-Williams he said that his memory was not to be compared with that of Professor Ernest Hughes, who on one memorable occasion recited an elaborate adjudication on an endless number of full length plays, dealing in detail with individual acts and scenes and speaking of the " characters " by name, as if they had been life-long friends of his.

11th March, 1952

In the night watches

HE must have been a sympathetic sort of fellow, for I saw him lighting a paraffin lamp as a night-light for the young tomato plants before shutting the greenhouse door and wishing them good night. Some of us who are older occasionally feel that a glimmer of light is sometimes a comfort when the night-watches seem rather longer than usual.

Indeed, I recently bought two of the stumpy candle variety for myself, though I must confess that as I asked for them I tried to look the benign old gentleman who was indulging his grandchildren.

Town dwellers who are not too fond of the utter dark are sometimes lucky in arriving at an understanding with an obliging street lamp. When we lived in Cardiff I arranged with the City Council to light up a beauty just outside the bedroom window, and that without paying any extra rate ; and as we then lived in the venetian blinds era you can imagine what interesting shadow patterns were worked out for me on the ceiling.

Not only could I count my imaginary sheep but if I opened my eyes I could see them actually negotiating the hurdles.

Here in our new home there is also a street lamp that does its best, but as it only has a curtain to play with it can't be expected to achieve many artistic effects.

You and I may be good sleepers, but during the occasional wakeful period that all mortal men know it is remarkable how interested we are in the passage of time. "What time is it, I wonder."

Perhaps there is no clock or watch in the room, or no light perhaps to see them by. But if it is winter-time and you are properly self-indulgent, there is still one expedient left you ; you send your toes nosing around for the hot-water bottle and try to calculate from the heat still remaining in it how far the night has gone.

I remember how amazed I was to see the late Puleston Jones, the blind preacher, taking out his watch half-way through his sermon and reading the time with his finger-tips. I must have forgotten how often I myself had performed the still more amazing feat of reading it with my toes.

1st *April*, 1952

The flaming knifeman

HE was cycling on the pavement, pedalling away for dear life, and in his hand was a flaming knife. I know it sounds sensationally lurid when put in print, but those who actually witnessed it hardly turned their eyes for a second look.

It was only a child or two on the opposite pavement, including myself, with no urgent errand on hand, who leisurely stopped to watch him, for though he pedalled so hard he still remained within view ; indeed, I have never seen a man who could move his legs so violently without moving at all.

He had so fixed his bicycle on an improvised wooden contraption that both wheels were held motionless, the only wheel that whirled round being the little grindstone fixed on the handlebar; and it was when he allowed the knife-blade to touch the stone that the flying sparks joined together to make a fine flame.

The knife, by the way, was already worn into a narrow stiletto and I feared that a few more touches on the stone would send it up in flames, leaving the cyclist with nothing but a black haft in his hands.

It was a biggish knife, and yet the nearest butcher's shop was at some distance, while the cyclist was actually just outside the door of a bank.

E

Ah, the Bank ! But somehow despite an occasional frown that I had seen behind the mahogany counter, I could hardly think it had quite come to that !

Dismissing all such sanguinary ideas, I allowed myself to enjoy to the full this picture, straight from a child's quainter-than-usual book of nursery rhymes.

He was certainly no ordinary cyclist, for though he pedalled so furiously he was not bent double over the handle-bars, but remained sitting majestically upright like a king on his throne or, to raise the pitch of my simile, like a county councillor in the Chair.

Not for him the singlet or sweater of a professional track-devourer but an almost ceremonial rig-out consisting of a longish black coat—I am not quite sure that he wore tails—and a staid bowler for a crown. The slightly drooping moustache, too, was so much in character that it seemed to be an integral part of the uniform.

8th April, 1952

Welsh wisdom

WHY should a collection of proverbs hold such a fascination for most people ? I remember how I revelled over the first Welsh collection that I came across.

When I was a boy, John Daniel Jones, of Hawen Hall, the witty, rhyming auctioneer of South Cardigan, presented me with the transactions of a Liverpool National Eisteddfod, and to me at the time much more interesting than the *awdl* and *pryddest* was the winning compilation of proverbs.

Had my boyish pencil-ticking really meant " reading, marking, and inwardly digesting," I had by this time surely been the exemplar of morals and the paragon of virtue, not to speak of attaining to that worldly wisdom which popular estimate, suggesting that it is chiefly confined to the stable and paddock, has designated " horse-sense."

It was Owen M. Edwards's *Cyfres y Fil* selection that now reminded me of that " Transactions " treasury, and once again my pencil has been busy with its ticking, although I realise that it is rather late in the day now to profit by the pieces of advice hidden in many a wise saw.

Sometimes the proverb is so old and shrivelled, like a wrinkled apple, that I cannot quite savour its meaning and yet I cannot help holding it long in my hand ; I feel that there is in it a whole orchard, a long green summer, and a misty, yellow autumn.

And in the very heart of it there is, too, a seed that can go to the making of a new orchard, blessed by a new summer and autumn.

Shall I pass on, in English, some of those proverbs which have claimed my pencil mark ? And as you read them it is more than likely that you will remember counterparts in other languages ; for wisdom was not born with the Cymry nor will it die with them.

Did you say that it is difficult for a man born in lowly circumstances to triumph over his traditions and environment and arrive at a higher social standing ? My proverb, agreeing with you, puts it succinctly in these few words—*"He born to a groat can't rise to fivepence."*

And, whether you are a fourpenny man or a fivepenny man, remember that the greater your ascent the more wary you will have to be, for " *the higher you climb the thinner the branches.*"

Our Welsh Solomon suggests one way of getting rid of a certain type of close-sticking " friend " and persistent visitor— " *Give a loan and lose a caller.*"

As we are on the subject of money one is reminded that " arian da a wrandewir " which, to give it its bare meaning stripped of its fine cynghanedd, asserts that " good money wins the ear."

Money or its equivalent must have played as great a part in the lives of our forefathers as it does in ours and it is often minted in our proverbs where the open handed is lauded and the close-fisted roundly castigated.

One proverb, embodying a truth more profoundly tragic than the biting cynicism of the others warns us that " Gold steals a man from himself."

When one notices with pain how somebody has completely altered for the worse one can only say that something has stolen him from himself, and Welsh proverbial lore points to gold as the arch-thief.

22nd April, 1952

The swallows were late

JOHN PUGH, the retired roadman, was riding his bicycle along the river bank, for since his accident he finds that riding is easier than walking. However, when he saw me, who am his pupil in bird lore, he managed to get off his bicycle : " They are behind schedule this year. They ought to be on this stretch of river by the eleventh or twelfth."

He was, of course, talking of the swallows, and for an old brush-and-barrow man what was more natural than he should have talked of a " stretch " of river ?

And with the word, almost as if they had overheard the " behind schedule " slander, three swallows swept along the water, almost like three children dashing to the school door before the bell has stopped. After all they were only three days late, and they had come a long way.

On a Sunday evening in a bus. Two women were evidently approaching their destination and they were doing their best to awaken a boy of four or five who had fallen fast asleep.

It was a difficult task. They even made the poor little fellow stand on his sleeping feet. They did their best and he seemed to be doing his best, but he simply couldn't wake up. At last a woman who sat just behind them leaned forward and handed the mother a sweet.

She put it between the sleeper's lips and a smile flickered on the child's beautiful face—and he opened his eyes.

I smiled, too, for I could not but remember seeing many a preacher, fighting with a somnolent congregation, after trying all sorts of things, at last bringing out of his bag of anecdotage a highly flavoured confection that seldom failed to do the trick.

24th June, 1952

Rosa Lloyd

A GIRL friend of hers brought her to my door, and it was the friend who had to open the interview and indeed do most of the talking.

" Would you be willing to marry her ? " A minister is never embarrassed by such a question for he knows by long hearing it that the request has merely to do with the performing of the marriage ceremony.

But I soon saw that there was some difficulty in their minds and not without a little diffidence came her further question, " Would it be all right, like, if she put a cross ? "

So that was the trouble : the bride-to-be, a young girl of 21, couldn't write. " No," I answered, immediately and dogmatically, almost as if I were quoting the statute book of English law, " it wouldn't be all right ; not for a young girl."

Both looked crestfallen and so I had to explain that the law of England might be satisfied with a cross, but I wasn't. " What would your ' in-laws ' think if they saw a fine young woman like you signing her name like that ?

" You say that you don't know your letters, but you have three clear weeks to learn. I won't be able to teach you to read and write in that time, but you come to me for half-an-hour on your way home from work every morning and you will be able to write ' Rosa Lloyd ' with a flourish."

And she came. It was rather pathetic to see her kneeling in front of a chair—for that is the posture that she chose—and patiently practising the mystic curves that somehow or other would mean " Rosa Lloyd " for the registrar.

The great morning arrived and I don't know which of us two was the more excited. It was a grand wedding. There were six bridesmaids dressed in the gayest of gay colours. She was in ivory white.

For the congregation the wedding was over with the pronouncing of the Benediction, but for her and me the great ordeal lay ahead in the vestry where the registrar waited with his two open books.

It was a cold day, and the ivory white didn't afford much protection, but that was not the only reason why the beautiful bride was visibly shivering.

Her anxious father made as if to take off his jacket to put over her shoulders, but she smilingly pushed him on one side and sat before the open books.

I looked over her shoulder and was relieved to find that " Rosa Lloyd " got on to both pages without hesitation. It was only I who noticed that in her other hand there was a crumpled scrap of paper.

I guessed what it was ; and when she secretly slipped it into my hand and I had an opportunity later of uncrumpling it, I read the two words, " Rosa Lloyd."

Poor girl, if in the excitement of the moment she had forgotten any of the mystic curves they would be there for her to take a sly peep at them.

29th July, 1952

Human limits

FOR those without specialist knowledge and interest, Helsinki will be remembered chiefly for that remarkable 100 metres photo-finish.

The second hands of four watches stopped dead over the very same decimal point, and but for the fact that a bright-eyed camera was posted at one end of the tape the coveted gold medal would have had to be cut into four !

One too graphic newspaperman announced that the race was " won by an eye-lash," but as a matter of fact eye-lashes can never win here even if they were as formidable as the tacked-on Hollywood specimens.

" Won by a shoulder-tip " is nearer the remark, though as it is the contact of tape and torso that really counts it would be a nice point to debate where torso ends and arm begins !

I look upon this result not as a remarkable coincidence but rather as further evidence that there seems to be a fairly definite mark beyond which human physical prowess cannot go.

One might have thought that somewhere or at some time there would be a startling exception where instead of knocking off an occasional tenth of a second in 100 metres a man knocks off, say, three or four seconds.

But at Helsinki, after sieving the runners of five continents, after intensive training, the fastest athletes when unaided by mechanical devices are forced to acknowledge that there is a mark, more or less fixed, where they hear the inexorable " thus far and no farther."

This rule, so evident in all spheres of unaided physical endeavour, does not seem to apply when we deal with the non-physical aspects of human life.

Is there any limit, for instance, to some people's gift of memory ? If somebody told me that Guto Nyth Bran ran a mile in two minutes I simply couldn't believe that my informant had his facts right, but if he related the strangest tales concerning a man's gift of memory or mathematical calculation, of art, or of music, though my natural surprise might lead me to demand further evidence, it would not result in a forthwith and forthright denial.

The child Mozart at his musical exercises set at naught all previous records. William Shakespeare's achievements can never be estimated by relating them to attempts in the same realm of dramatising.

And so with character, with moral goodness or badness. Here again there seems to be no limit to human achievement in either direction.

No four stop-watches could ever unite in saying—" There it is : human nature cannot do better or do worse than that."

The four men of the photo-finish were not just a quartette who happened to be endowed by nature with legs that moved faster than other people's.

Nature's gift had been developed by years of constant training, by systematic coaching and endless practice.

It was the great Nurmi who lit the torch at Helsinki, and I often remember the quiet confidence of his running days when, referring to the fact that some competitors at some point of the race would forge far ahead of him, he remarked—" They always come back to me."

They always did ; and that was possibly why he had got into the way of striding along as if he were the only man on the track, calmly consulting his wrist-watch at the end of every lap.

He knew the time that he ought to take for each, so that really his only fellow competitor was Nurmi at his best.

You and I know what it is to be hurried and flurried by fellow runners who seem to be getting all the claps when we might as well recognise just what we are capable of doing and keep jogging along with unperturbed minds and an occasional peep at our left wrist.

23rd September, 1952

September frolic

MORE than once when I have seen a crow standing all alone in a field I have felt that it was the beginning of a new Æsop's fable. Indeed, before now I have found myself trying to wonder how the story goes and whether it is a fox or a goat that was about to jump over the hedge to carry on the tale. But Æsop is long dead and the crows have forgotten how to talk.

That is not to say that the fields have lost all their surprises. During an early morning walk only last week I had occasion to rub my eyes—metaphorically it is true, for as a matter of plain prose both hands were in their proper place, the depths of my pockets ! The path led through the middle of the field, a perfectly flat field but for the yard or two which sloped down to the river, about 50 paces to my right. It was on that sloping bank that something was afoot. I couldn't make head or tail of it, not head or tail or body. Was it one or many ? Was it fish or fowl ? But for the fact that it was well out of the water I should almost have voted for a new kind of grey fish. Did otters jump about ? I ought to say that I could only catch an occasional glimpse when the whatever it was leapt to the level of the field. One would have thought of sporting hares but that the colour was definitely silver grey in the morning light. I was now, of course, making quietly for the river bank and wishing that I had a sounder pair of shoes, for the grass was long and heavy with drew. No, there was no magic climax. They were two or three or more grey squirrels dashing back and fore like mad, leaping and careering round as if there were never to be any more September mornings. As I came upon them one leapt down from one tree and up another and soon all had become part of the quiet grey leaves.

In a day or two the whole scene had very much changed, or, to be exact, it was altogether a different scene, for I now found myself on a cliff overlooking St. Catherine's Fort in Tenby. I shall agree with you that one could hardly find a more quiet spot and yet the real charm of the sea to-day is its unceasing restlessness. The gulls, too, borrowing the sea's prevailing tone of grey and white have also caught its restlessness. Occasionally they stand together in solemn conclave and then suddenly away they go as if an urgent wire had arrived and there was good treasure for the first to arrive, and as they go they start another competition seeking to find whose voice it is that most nearly approaches the authentic B.B.C. studio gull.

In the midst of all this movement of waves and of wings there was something in the air right above the fort that was quite still, so still that it almost frightened me. The wings were not the two curves of the gull, so accommodating to the child artist's pencil, but two taut straight lines like the brows of an angered man. That great hawk, perched motionless on some invisible ledge of air, was a menace to everything that dared move, a leaping wave, a wheeling gull, a man's beating heart.

30*th September*, 1952

Seats of learning

THOSE of you who are familiar with the South Beach at Tenby will remember the steep concrete path that leads you to it. One morning I saw two or three schoolboys coming up to meet me there as I was about to go " down to the sea," and I was rather pleased to notice that each one of them had a book in his hand.

Isn't it good to find children who even at holiday-time cling to their books ? Their volumes didn't appear to be text-books, but they all looked pretty solid, and, lifting my eyes from the books to the boys' faces, I saw how this love of reading was reflected in each studious countenance.

I even turned round to look after them. And they looked after me. And no wonder, for, did I know it, they were patiently waiting for me to reach the bottom of the little hill.

Each boy was carrying a single roller-skate as well as a book, and when I saw them place book on skate and then prepare to sit on the hefty volume I knew it was time for me to get clear of the speedway !

It was well worth seeing them rattling down that slope, with feet well up and steering arms spread-eagled in the wind, each boy a potential Freddy Williams.

In future when people refer to " seats of learning " I fear that one mind will turn to that concrete slope and the indispensable books.

Many a warm afternoon tempted bathers into the water and from all outward and visible signs they enjoyed the experience, but I must confess that I once shivered vicariously as, from my bedroom window, I followed an intrepid early morning bather down to the North Beach.

He only wore a bath-towel over his bathing suit and leaving that on the sand and slipping off his shoes he trotted off manfully to the cold edge of the water.

Anyone could tell that it was a matter of conscience with him, but waning resolution slackened his pace as he got nearer the danger zone and it was a very hesitant, tentative toe that tasted the rippling water's first chill.

But in he went, stepping high like a Llwyncadfor pony. Hadn't he made up his mind that he would take his morning bathe and one must not let one's self down ?   Moreover, for all I knew there may have been watchful, admiring eyes at some other bedroom window, and what gallant knight can afford to disappoint his gallery ?

The water has only just covered his knees, but he halts, possibly gasping with cold. He stoops, cupping his hands, and then, reverently baptises his bald head, finding it at the moment more convenient to subscribe to the sprinkling tradition rather than the total immersion school.

I was almost as relieved as he must have been when he at last turned his back on the Atlantic and raced stiffly, but much more zestfully now, back to the waiting towel and shoes and up, I hope, to a warm room and a properly appreciative wife.

7th October, 1952

The old man of Henllan

HUNDREDS of years ago the " Old Man of Pencader " assured a King of England that in his corner of the world the Cymric tongue would always thrive ; and last week *Plaid Cymru* planted in Pencader's soil a picture of that prophecy in solid granite.

It was fitting that the huge block should have been quarried in North Wales for both Gwynedd and Deheubarth claim a part in that prophecy, and Gwynfor, the trusted commander-in-chief, admitted this all-Wales claim when he called upon William George, the Prince of Arfon, to unveil the monument while Dyfnallt, Prince of Mid-Wales, and others were invited to add their further eloquent appeals.

The thousands present were deeply moved, and one can only hope that the enthusiasm engendered has in it something of the enduring assurance of the prophet, and that every word was cut in granite.

But Pencader had its sad story, too, for a few days previously the British Railways, wielding a ruthless, unsentimental axe, had lopped off its Newcastle Emlyn branch because—so they averred —it no longer bore fruit.

One agrees that of late years it was only a most select company that was privileged to travel those enchanted miles through Llandyssul, Pentre Cwrt and Henllan. There were but two or three coaches all told, and it often happened that this meant a coach for each passenger, such was the high standard of luxury provided.

And there was never any unbecoming hurry. I always had time to admire the inevitable leisurely heron at Allt y Cafan pool, and that lone dreamer must have felt that the passing train, although a little bit noisy, belonged to his own world of contemplative meandering.

Pentre Cwrt Halt is only a matter of a few yards of single platform, but it, too, has its story. A farmer and his wife had just alighted there one Friday evening after a visit to the Newcastle Emlyn mart, and the good man would not allow his own wife even to imagine that he had ever taken a drop too much.

But when he got off the train and was making for the wrong direction, turning his back on the one and only exit, his wife had to put him right and it was rather pathetic to hear the poor old fellow excusing himself and muttering, " Hen stesion fach ddryslyd iawn yw hon." (" A very confusing little station, this.")

For many years of my life it was from Henllan Station that I set forth on all my never very distant journeys. To catch the only train that would take my brothers and myself to college, to Cardiff, to Aberystwyth, to Bangor and to Edinburgh, we had to leave home for Henllan in the early morning, and during the winter sessions it would of course be pitch dark.

I remember one occasion when my brother and I had safely caught the train at Henllan and had waited an hour or so at Pencader for the North Wales train, our senses were so numbed with cold that we entered the wrong train and found ourselves back in Henllan again to trudge the four mile climb home.

Travelling in winter in those days was a Spartan test of endurance, and do what you would you could never persuade your thin blood to travel all the way to your toes. You were lucky if you found a hot water metal container under your seat, but by the time you had been tugged and jerked along the bleak coast of North Wales the water no longer pretended to be any different from the rest of us.

Indeed, miles before arriving at Afon Wen, most passengers were beginning to be altruistic enough to share their " hot-water " comforters with their fellows !

Henllan was the only place in the whole countryside where the clock really mattered. Even in chapel, though the minister was a stickler for punctuality, allowances had to be made for watches that told different tales.

So that when it was a matter of catching a train at Henllan one had to be on the safe side, and it was not unusual to hear a scrap of conversation like this, " Yes, I caught it right enough, but I had only been on the station for 20 minutes when the train arrived " —meaning that the speaker had cut it rather fine.

You can still get to Henllan from Pencader, but no longer in your own compartment and your own coach. One can see new roadside scenes, but it will be useless to look out for the blue heron and the blue pool of Teifi, not to speak of the grand good fellowship of drivers, guards and porters.

I realise now how big a part sentiment had played in holding me between the two rails that would bring me to the old Henllan, scene of so many happy homecomings and so many goodbyes, some of them tragically sad during the war years. Now the British Railways have left the Old Man of Henllan no option, and I must climb into the bus like the rest of you.

14th October, 1952

The long handle

A PLUMBER and his apprentice, a stonemason, and a carpenter were all intent on the job of persuading one pipe to release its hold on another. But the two pipes had struck up a friendship when the house was first built, and as the alliance had been cemented by the gripping memories of many years it was not by a mere touch of the hand that the ancient bond was to be broken.

Many trusty tools were tried ; even the hammer was called upon to tap away the outer paint and to disturb the inner rust. There were iron-jawed grips above and below : sometimes four determined men strove separately and then joined together in a sudden co-operative pull, two on the clockwise trail and two on the anti-clock.

I looked on, the only help I could give being an occasional involuntary explosive sigh that coincided with their peak effort, a sigh that would do credit to the B.B.C. repertory grunt that audibly registers a tremendous studio pull or lift.

But even my moral help availed them nothing. The ancient allegiance held firm. Then up spake the master-plumber : " One of you get the iron tubing." The length of tubing was duly fitted over the handle of the spanner and with the extra leverage of this longer handle the impossible was at last accomplished.

The quick eyes of four accomplished artists at once noted the—to me—imperceptible, infinitesimal first movement and in a very little time the years-old alliance of two pipes was broken by the sly intervention of an alien traitor pipe.

Had I to name this stratagem, using the modern military nomenclature, I should have termed it, " Operation Long Handle."

As soon as a new star of scientific wisdom swims into my ken I immediately think of hitching my creaking wagon to it. I remembered the old-fashioned gas-tap in the bedroom grate.

It was so stiff that it was only with a supreme struggle that it could be manipulated at all. One had thought of oiling it well, but then, with so many children about the house, a too easy tap would constitute actual danger.

With the fresh ardour of the scientific inventor I went upstairs carrying in my hand a yard of brass tubing. It fitted perfectly, and now, if in the dead of night my thought turns to cups of tea, I have only to fit in my magic tube and with the lazy touch of a finger, and with no back-bending, the gas is ready to perform its act of benevolence.

Then, as I sip my tea I toy with the idea of becoming a spare-time plumbing expert, strictly as an amateur, of course, for I know what an exclusive body the professional fraternity is.

I wish I could lay my hands on a most interesting travel book that I once read, for I should like to be able to quote the exact words that described the peasants of Cardiganshire as seen by a stranger about 100 years ago.

Among other things he mentioned the uncommon type of spade used. He had never seen a smaller spade nor a longer handle.

I smiled as I wondered whether the writer was unconsciously summing up a gallant county's character, the tiny spade speaking of the actual amount of work done, while the far-reaching handle made a brave show.

But to-day, after my first plumbing lesson, I see that Cardigan knew what it was about even then ; the long handle not only saved the peasant much needless backbending but used skilfully, with the region above the left knee an easy fulcrum, it gave that leverage which like faith can remove mountains.

The readers of Neville Cardus invariably connect " the long handle " with a cricket pitch, but it can be attached to water pipes, a gas tap, and a spade in a Cardiganshire field.

Ink and inspiration

ONCE again I had come to the bottom of the page, but as the ink on the last three or four lines was still wet I couldn't very well turn over.

" But," you will ask, " where was the blotting paper ? " I only wish that I knew. The blotting paper and I are forever losing one another, and I am not at all prepared to admit that the fault is always on one side.

Whether you blame me or blame the blotter, all I know is that it rather shatters the inspiration, if any, when a writer has to stop in midstride in order to shuffle all the heaps of paper within reach, or, worse still, if he has to push back his chair and get up to rummage on the mantelpiece or the piano.

The only mitigating aspect of the whole procedure is that even though the quest is fruitless, as it so often is, when one returns to the chair the lines are dry enough ; as dry as the disturbed fount of inspiration.

So often is this ritual observed in my room that I might almost confess that the perambulating quest is in actual practice my one unfailing sheet of blotting paper.

Those who bother to read what I write week by week may have noticed that the more arid paragraphs occur at fairly regular intervals, and did they consult my manuscript they would discover that these are actually the beginnings of new pages, when I have to scratch my head all over again after having resumed my chair.

Sometimes when I have a feeling almost amounting to dead certainty that the elusive sheet is going to beat me in the game of hide and seek, refusing to budge from my chair, I practise quite another technique. This, I ought to explain, can only come off on very cold days when my room indulges in a fire, either one that burns electricity or, better still, honest coal.

Need I say that the chair is as near as possible to the said fire, and one has only to toast the page for a few seconds to find that during that short time not only is the ink perfectly dry but, stimulated by the heat, the sluggish bloodstream in my hand finds its way to the white tips of my fingers.

On a fireless day in similar circumstances I have seen myself trying to achieve the same result by waving the paper in air as if it were the white flag of a beaten army. That plan, too, works, though it takes an appreciably longer period and, unfortunately, by the time I have given up waving the white flag my halted writing has often acknowledged complete surrender.

Because of faith

*Or who shut up the sea with doors when it brake forth . . . .
and brake up for it my decreed place, and set bars and doors ;
and said, " Hitherto shalt thou come, but no further ; and
here shall thy proud waves be stayed "*

IT is when the doors are occasionally pushed open, with calamitous results, that we bethink ourselves of the overwhelming might of certain natural elements. To Job the *closed* door was the amazing thing. Living on an island, a very tiny one amid the immense wastes of water, it is strange that almost for a life time we can take these mighty doors for granted, apparently quite satisfied that all the waves of ocean have heard that quiet " hitherto " uttered in the morning of time : heard it and accepted it.

We say that we have no faith, but I have watched masons building a bungalow practically on the beach at Borth, and whistling as they worked. They must know, of course, that an occasional high tide will sweep across the dividing road and they will probably add a storm shutter to the dront door that can be fitted should necessity arise. They agree that the sea may swirl up several yards above its usual high tide mark, not realising how marvellous it is that they can think in yards so contentedly when the sea reaches back for thousands of miles.

Were the Atlantic in a forgetful mood to ignore that " hitherto " which has for so long been ringing in its ears, one could well imagine it rushing along not for yards but for miles and miles before remembering and pulling up.

Indeed, one could well imagine the complete swamping of the British Isles in one night's forgetfulness, leaving for the eyes of morning nothing but an occasional mountain top above the calm waste of water. We perhaps smile at the idea, and we bring out our science primers to attempt to prove that there is logic in our smile. But really there is no logic in it apart from the logic of simple faith.

Science at best only notes what happens and how one thing follows another, and has so followed it for as long as man remembers. If we think of this and kindred matters at all what really upholds us is a sort of feeling that surely the something or somebody that is in charge will keep things going ; it or he will not drown a whole Continent, just as it or he will not allow harvests to fail all over the world.

But why are we so sure ? " Well, if not," we argue, " that would prove either that the Power doesn't care for us, or, caring, that it can't help us."

But why are men everywhere so sure that the Power is at all eager to help us, or being eager that it *can* help us ? Why do we take it for granted that all the multifarious things that go to make up a universe—winds, waves, trees, animals, stars and suns and men—can never get out of hand ? How is it, for instance, that the moon's eclipse the other night was scheduled in my pocket diary printed last year.

The bare fact is that we do take it all for granted ; we can't really imagine the whole thing getting into a complete tangle, and though we realise that it is not enough to refer to the transcending Power merely in terms of finite human personality, we are certain that " He " is nearer the mark than " it " when we stand amazed before the dove-tailed orderliness and beneficence of the universe.

Even as we grieve over the terrible devastation caused by the momentary opening of the door we thank God that there *is* a door and that a whole universe has caught the word " hitherto."

One evening last summer I was walking alone along the shores of Cardigan Bay. At the turn of the tide the ebb had left its thin strip of foam along the beach and I couldn't help contrasting the ease of the operation with that of the toiling groundsman at Newbridge fields pushing along his heavy little contraption on a Saturday morning to mark out the touchlines for the afternoon football.

It was amazing to think that this white line on the beach, built of nothing more substantial than airy foam, was to be recognised by the hefty, bustling, Atlantic forwards, even when the game was at its roughest, as their inexorable boundary line ; and that the ball could not get over it without the frantic waving of many flags.

Did we know it, it is because of faith, that despite the desolation of the occasional storm, men will continue to build on the very edge of ocean, and whistle as they build. The whistled tune may be just the latest music-hall ditty but, for all that, it is a great hymn of faith.

And equally as important as this confidence in the general ordering of natural forces is the unexpressed confidence in certain moral and spiritual forces that dwell in men's hearts. Just as the very fact that we were all so shocked when we read of the sea's door-opening on the East Coast only showed what implicit confidence we had placed on God's doors for all the years, in the same way the shock we knew when we read of the looting by a despicable handful only showed our deep-rooted acceptance of the fact that men would of course help the distressed.

The looting made news ; it was the exceptional that proved how we take the rule for granted, that man in God's image will instinctively want to help even to the point of grave personal danger and willing sacrifice.

What a boon it would be if statesmen everywhere would build on that ; they could then afford to whistle on the job.

24th February, 1953

Ben Bowen

IT is good to know that Treorchy schools are preparing to commemorate the 75th anniversary of the late Ben Bowen's birth ; and Treorchy and the Rhondda generally can with an easy conscience spread flowers on the poet's grave for they gave him flowers in plenty during his short but strenuous life of 24 years.

They rallied round the gifted collier boy with typical Rhondda hero-worship and when his health was at breaking point they found means to send him all the way to South Africa. It was when he arrived home from that vain search for healing that I saw him for the first and only time, and I shall always be grateful to Dyfnallt, his firm friend, for introducing me to him as we stood outside the old Bala-Bangor College.

What I remember is a shock of red hair, a pale face, and the two brightest eyes that ever looked out on the world.

I often wonder what Ben Bowen's poetry would have been like had he been born into this present age. Even in his own day, despite his youth and his inexperience, he was a daring experimenter.

It was only last year, at Aberystwyth, that the Eisteddfod authorities granted candidates for the Chair the right to take certain liberties when handling the cast-iron rules of the 24 metres, not to ignore the rules, but to obey them as true literary artists and to further develop with imagination their inherent musical possibilities.

That is exactly what Ben did 50 years ago when he submitted his awdl. Again when he wrote free verse his adventurous muse sometimes took great liberties with metrical forms ; so much so that some readers regarded many a verse of his as being hardly separated from plain prose, and there were not many adjudicators in the Wales of 1900 who could be as brave as Elfed in awarding a prize to Ben's " Goleuni y Byd " (" The Light of the World ").

To give readers who do not understand Welsh some idea of that poem, I have tried to translate a few of its lines, and I imagine that even this approximation to the original will impress, especially when one remembers that the author was so young :

Like an ode in the poet's mind,
One endless music growing eternally beautiful
In the air of a purer world,
So in God's mind
The creation grows and lives.

The light's flood, as it billows down,
Foams into all colours,
And the mountain arises from dawn's baptism
Dripping with God.

Dawn journeys forth at the beckoning of an eye,
And both have understood one another
To a nicety;
And God, for whom the suns are but the bells
on the hem of His garment,
In the blue vastnesses,
Holds man to the path of law
As he ever seeks revelation.

Man, like Moses, craves to see
The tempest of immortal glory
That sleeps like a child
On the arms everlasting.
What is to-day's black hell
But the shadow of God's Throne
In the clear shining of that light
That knits with the living rays' needles
The mantle of the lily's sanctity?

Light of the world,
To-night thy gentle kiss
Will touch the young cheeks of the stars,
Smiling on God's knees,
Not yet having learnt to walk.

3rd March, 1953

Black and white

Oll yn eu gynau gwynion
Ac ar eu newydd wedd,
Yn debyg idd eu Harglwydd
Yn dod i'r lan o'r bedd.

" ALL in their robes of white, like their Lord, arising from
the grave" That is the oft-repeated refrain of the Welsh
hymn that at funeral after funeral seeks to light up the gloom of an
open grave; but at Merthyr Mawr to-day I hear the words as
Cynan once heard them, for I, too, am looking not at a black-coated
group of mourners but at gleaming patches of snowdrops among
the graves, " all in their robes of white."

It is to St. Donat's that the snowdrops come first to the Vale, but here, too, at Merthyr Mawr, they come early, and when they arrive they arrive in crowds. Here and in the nearby woods one has an Alice in Wonderland feeling when one finds so many trees casting white shadows on the enchanted ground.

The rooks' chorus, at this time of the year a most pleasant and heartening sound, suggests that a great number must have congregated together at no great distance from the church, but the only ones I notice in the field are not " ones " at all but " twos." As yet the alliance, " for better, for worse " is perhaps only at its tentative stage, for I do not see any of the orthodox wounded-wing demonstrations where the poor love-lorn hopeful tries to show how sorely stricken he is. The one looks as unconcerned as the other while they step out foraging for food, but I notice that each pair keeps together.

Apart from an occasional splutter of crocus flame there is very little colour here to-day, but, even so, Merthyr Mawr's spring study in black and white is very worthwhile.

The account of von Rundstedt's death reminds me of the afternoon when I met two—or was it three?—German officer-prisoners here at Merthyr Mawr. They were gazing at the beautiful churchyard from the road where they stood, and when I came along they had a question to put to me.

Strangely enough, not one of them could speak English and, which is not at all strange, I knew no German. At last I understood that what had taken their attention was a small block of stone near the wall that seemed to me to be the pedestal perhaps of some vanished column. They had wondered whether it was a child's gravestone.

Wherever those men are to-day, they and hundreds of their fellow prisoners must be still cherishing the memory of this beautiful countryside ; and I hardly believe that they can think harshly of the men and women whom they met here.

The story of the Island Farm Camp will one day be fraught with much interest to the historian, and it would be as well if somebody who knows it all were to buy a writing pen and a fat notebook now ; for ink outlasts memory.

Bridgend's reactions knew two stages, or perhaps three. When the prisoners arrived they were objects of much hate and our loyal citizens could not understand why such dangerous people should be planted so near ; and during that clever tunnelling and and mighty getaway some of the more timid among us were terrified. Then came the middle period when public opinion was satisfied that among the hundreds there might be some who were not so bad ; and when the prisoners were at last allowed a great measure of freedom, and mingled with people on the streets and in the churches, there was a remarkable swing of the pendulum.

The doors of many homes were opened wide, and some of those who had anathematised most violently now spoke almost as extremely again, but this time to another tune.

Von Rundstedt was pointed out to me when he was being taken for hospital treatment, but by to-day one has forgotten the names of the many soldiers, some of them high-ranking, whom one met. It was an ordinary private that I once met in the woods near the ruins of Candleston Castle. I am no Sherlock Holmes, but when I saw a piece of cardboard half hidden under his coat, knowing the signs, I asked him if he was fond of water-colours.

He was all enthusiasm, and he showed me the cardboard and the pitifully-inadequate piece of paper that he had drawing-pinned on to it. When I supplied him with some more suitable material he later sent to me a very lively sketch of a cottage in Gower near the camp to which he had been removed. Another artist presented me with two or three samples of his work, but instead of painting the Merthyr Mawr scene he preferred to allow his " hiraeth " to picture in imagination the wooded hills of his far homeland.

It all seems so long ago. The world has changed ; allies who were then lauded to the skies have become inhuman monsters, while the one-time monsters are drilled to stand between us and the new enemies. The one changeless element is this sense of international suspicion which feeds the insatiable furnaces of war preparation, each nation firmly proclaiming, and possibly believing, that it acts merely in self-defence.

When I at last enter the door of the little church, on which the rector has pinned a written invitation reminding me that this is my Father's House and that I can enter without knocking, I do not pretend that I go in to pray in the sense that I mentally frame any petition, but I sit there quietly feeling more certain than ever of one or two things.

17th March, 1953
' The glory is departed '

IN an old travel book " A Tour through Wales," I came across this description of a certain Glamorgan town, but when I copy it here I shall leave the town unnamed to see if you can guess its identity.

" The landscape about—is exceedingly rich : the mountains, the river, and its woody banks, form a beautiful back-ground and contrast to the bold and craggy shore, and the broken and insulated Knoles near it.

" Just above the ferry is the seat of Mr. Vernon, situated in the centre of this enchanted view.

"The sea-breezes from the Bristol Channel have no influence over the verdure of the trees on this southern coast, which flourish as well here as in the more inland parts."

Possibly the word "ferry" gave you a profitable clue, but there was little else in the description to suggest that the tourist—whose name I don't know, as the fly-leaf is missing—was talking of Briton Ferry; at any rate, not the Briton Ferry we see as our bus weaves its cumbersome way through the busy main street.

Strangely enough, without looking for it, I found further references to the same town in another book, written 150 years ago "by the Rev. J. Evans, B.A., late of Jesus College, Oxon," which corroborates all the glowing things said by the earlier tourist:

"Here is the justly admired spot called Britton Ferry. The advantages which nature has bestowed on this place baffle all attempts at adequate description; whatever enters into the bold or pleasing landscape, are here combined, verdant slopes, shady woods, abrupt declivities, with massy oaks growing out of the iron-stone rocks; and showing their roots through the strata on the banks of the river; the River Nedd opening in a wide estuary to the ocean: the moving scene of shipping up and down the river; all unite to adorn this place with numerous and peculiar charms."

One summer afternoon when I walked the wooded slopes above Briton Ferry I felt that the glory had not all departed, but that was not my feeling when on a recent visit two young people met my train and escorted me to a meeting at some distance from the station.

They took me along certain back ways from which occasional tunnel-like alleys branched out; we went under a dark bridge and stepped gingerly over metal plates to have a peep at the old docks and the new bridge looming black in the distance. A fine chapel mounted guard on our right, standing apparently right in the middle of the tinplate works.

"Indeed," protests John Evans. "It must be a perverted one indeed, that could despoil nature of many of the beauties she has so lavishly bestowed on Briton Ferry."

And yet, almost in the same breath, speaking of the continuation of the Neath Canal, he admits that "beauty should be subordinate to utility; and in many instances taste has been obliged by imperious necessity to make sacrifices, which though she does not admire, she has been unable to avoid."

Little did John Evans realise that it was the beginning of the end, and had his ghost joined us that night as we picked our way to the docks I don't know what words he would be muttering to himself, though I imagine that one of them would be that despairing sigh of doom, *Ichabod*, the glory is departed.

A tune of their own

ON Saturday evenings right through the winter you may have been listening to the football results given over the wireless. I, too, have sometimes heard them, but I have been keeping my ears open not so much for the results as for the announcer's tune. I feel certain that the announcer himself has not deliberately sat down to compose the tune, but he sings it nevertheless, and he sings it well, especially when the soccer list is being chanted.

The first team named and its particular score are given in a monotone, but the name of the second team always has its special rising or falling notes, the musical run depending, if not on the run of the play, definitely on the result of the game. That is why, before the actual goal score is given, I am always able to say whether the second team won or lost or drew.

I can hear him, in imagination, now : " The first team, two goals ; the second team . . . " How did he intone " the second team " ? He may introduce one tune which my well-trained ear interprets as " and the second team *also* " ; so he needn't have bothered to tell me that it, too, scored two goals, like team number one. That was his " draw " tune. When the second team has won, though I am not able to say by how many goals it has achieved victory, the tune has already announced the win. It is as clear as if he had actually said, " The first team, two goals ; but the second team did even better. . . . " The draw and the win for the second team are each musically telegraphed before the actual figures are announced ; but when team number two has come a cropper, you will instantly note the absence of these two tunes.

This time it is the first team named that has a slight lift to the end of its monotone while poor number two is given nothing but the flat notes of the doomed.

Alun Davies and other experienced sports announcers, though they may not have been aware of it, have been *singing* football results for all these years. If you doubt that there is a tune just ask an inexperienced announcer to read the list, and though the figures are correct, you will at once miss the enthusiasm and confidence and long use that has all the right notes as well as all the right answers.

To discuss intonation on paper is almost impossible. Have I not seen eager biographers trying to tell readers what their hero-preacher's *hwyl* sounded like ?—trying and failing miserably, because, for one thing, there are so many shades of sounds packed in tightly between the nearest notes that our scale recognises ; and because each of these particular shades again has its own emotional stress. Intonation is hard to describe, but nevertheless all-important.

I was once in a room at some distance from the kitchen where the radio was on. I could hear it but could make out no word of what was being said. I had no watch and wondered whether it was just after eight or just before ; " No, it isn't eight," I said to myself, " the news hasn't started : this is the ' Lift Up Your Hearts '." It was only later that I realised how the intonation, minus any words, had told me the whole thing. It is more than likely that the preacher, whoever he was, fondly imagined that he had succeeded in capturing the matter-of-fact tones of the news reader, but one could spot the difference through two thicknesses of wall. Any moral appeal seems to demand a tune of its own.

That is why, even when we have *the very words* uttered on some particular occasion, we can never be quite sure ; we have the words but we didn't see the speaker's face when he pronounced them and, just as important, we didn't hear the tune to which they were sung. " What is truth? " asked a certain ruler-judge on his bench, but Biblical expositors would know how to deal with the words if only the chronicler knew how to report intonation as well as words.

" And would not stay for an answer," so Lord Bacon ventures to comment, but perhaps Pilate did stay for an answer ; the answer that refused to come. Were one presented with the tune as well as the words one could hope to decide whether Pilate was genuinely seeking for information from one who he recognised was able to give him light on the subject or whether his words, though in question form, were just a convenient vessel into which he could pour the impatient scorn of the learned Roman for this Jew who babbled of truth.

This is but one instance of many that could be recalled and they occur not only on the pages of a history book, but on the as yet unwritten pages of to-day's reported gossip. " Yes, those were the very words he used, and I'm not going to forgive him ! " Dear Sir or Madam, perhaps you would find it easier to forgive if the tale-bearer could reproduce the exact intonation as well as the exact words—or indeed you might find it still harder.

12th May, 1953

Colour question

IF the accommodating reader is well versed in psychology he will greatly oblige me by fitting in the suitable philosophic terms, not merely to adorn my little tale but to give it necessary body and significance. Otherwise what I have to say may become a mere string of frivolous anecdotes, each one of them true enough, but, deprived of the help I crave, having no truth worth proclaiming.

Here is the first. Addressing a woman whom I had not seen for some time I ventured to remark how well she looked. She pointed a finger to each of her cheeks in turn and answered, with a smile, " Well, I try to make myself look well." It was only then that my innocent eye realised that she had certainly been helping nature to grow its roses, and that with sensitive artistry.

But it was what she added that seemed to call for a psychological corollary : " It is rather strange, but when I am feeling below par I put on a little extra colour, and I immediately feel better." I had always thought the roses *followed* good health, but am I to believe now that good health follows the roses, even when they are artificial blooms ?

This next carries with it still deeper psychological implications, deeper but not altogether unrelated to the first instance. Pupils at a girls' school were engaged in a not unusual pastime—a frank and uninhibited discussion of their teacher's idiosyncrasies.

On this occasion it was a certain woman teacher who claimed the forum's attention, and this gem was part of the judicial summing-up, " Have you noticed that when she's got that white silk blouse on she's not at all bad ? "

How often have we been taught that it isn't the cowl that makes a monk ; but I shall never feel quite as certain about that now, for a black cowl and a white blouse belong to the same category and, for all I know, may have similar magical qualities.

When I am feeling run down I can't imagine the psychiatrist prescribing a tube of colour for my cheek's yellowed vellum but when I am showing signs of being hyper-critical and miserably censorious it is possible that he will tell me that what I really need is not a new measure of Christian charity or a new book on social conduct but a new hat or a new tie.

When speakers don't seem quite certain as to the correct sequence of cause and effect we pull them up by reminding them that they put " the cart before the horse." But one is not so convinced of the proverb's aptness when one has to look twice to find out whether the horse pulls the cart or the cart pushes the horse.

The more I think about it the more readily do the examples crowd in. I cannot vouch for the accuracy of the following, but I can assure my psychological assistant—who I hope has kept up with my meandering thus far—that it is an accurate chronicle of what was reported to me by a West Walian.

A young woman who was to attend a relative's funeral had been refused a new dress, fitting for the occasion, and when she returned home that evening she was in no mood to dilate regarding the day's proceedings and her answers were on the short side.

" Was the family very upset ? "   " Yes, they cried a lot."
" Did you cry ? "   " How could I cry in a navy blue costume ?"

Her peevish rhetorical question almost gives rise to a more fundamental query—Do we wear mourning because we cry, or do we cry because we wear mourning? Were we armed with the necessary academic weapons quite a battle could be waged on that particular field of psychology, and indeed its issue might well affect the practical politics of our everyday life and behaviour.

And again we are in West Wales. When the local veterinary surgeon had been summoned to attend to an ailing cow he told the cowman that it was a serious case, but if he and his helpers would follow his instructions carefully there was every hope for a complete cure.

He first inquired whether a certain kind of tree grew on the land : they were to pick a quantity of leaves which were then to be boiled. When the resulting liquid had cooled sufficiently it was to be applied three times a day, and after each application the affected part was to be washed thoroughly in clean water.

When the farmer, who was an intimate friend, asked the vet. what property the leaves possessed he was told that they were brought into the picture simply to make sure that the udder was washed thoroughly three times a day : " Men will never believe that clean water can do the job but they will enjoy hunting for those magic leaves."

In a way of speaking, the cooled leaf-water was there to wash the cowman's eyes with !

Even without being a schooled psychologist one could venture on the assertion that it is not merely in the vet's surgery that eye-wash is bottled ; it is to be found on all sorts of shelves, and most of us swear by it in some form or other. And it still works its miracles.

19*th May*, 1953
Choristers

IF I take a wrong road on to-day's peregrination you must blame the chubby index finger of a little girl who, one of three, sat right in front of me in a Swansea Valley chapel. The service hadn't started—indeed, the organist hadn't yet arrived, and the three little girls, whoever they were, patiently and silently waited.

Presently I noticed one of them lifting up her hand, but not high enough to be seen by those in front, and pointing at something. I know it was only meant for her two pals, but I, too, ran my eyes along that finger and from its tip they took a flying leap in the direction indicated—just above the organ pipes.

At first I saw nothing, but then I, too, saw the little robin perched on one of the pipes.

With that the organist arrived and I wondered what the red-breast's reaction would be to the first blast emanating from the pipes. But his playing was mercifully as soft as the whispering of the wind, and Master Robin paid no more heed than he would have given the rustling of leaves in the wood.

During the opening voluntary he more than once appeared as if he were about to take wing, but each time, thinking better of it, he stayed on to see whether the choir was in good voice.

Then having satisfied himself on that score—this time a musical one !—instead of flying out through the hole in the high window pane he dived through the loop of the red curtain that separated church from Sunday-school.

It was afterwards that I learnt of the nest above the cupboard although I might have guessed it by the way another robin joined forces, flying in and out through the window and the curtain loop.

Though these red-breasted parents were to be commended for showing such eagerness to have their children well brought up in Sunday-school I couldn't but experience a certain trade-union fellow-feeling for the preacher whose fine sermon had to compete with the weaving of busy wings.

26th May, 1953

The flags are out

ALMOST would one say that the very winds are tinted red, white and blue with the way that they are playing about with Union Jacks.

One can almost hear the questioning windy whispers : " What is all this about ? We are accustomed to the green foliage on the trees but these new-fangled multicoloured square leaves that have grown overnight on straight, white, branchless tree-trunks are a puzzle for us.

" And not only do they grow on trees but they spring out everywhere, on the tops of houses and hitherto bare walls, and they have even struck root on the fast-rushing cars where we would hardly expect them to find foothold. We push them about, we turn them over and give them a good shaking, but as yet we haven't fathomed the mystery."

It isn't the winds only who are amazed and almost bewildered by this sudden burgeoning of red, white and blue leafage on a soil that foreigners regard as being unresponsive to a degree.

It is strange how the word " flag " is made to stand for two things that couldn't be more different, the one from the other. A bit of canvas fluttering to every breath of air is a " flag " : so is a solid slab of stone.

You have to look up at the one : it is there high above your head. The other is under your foot. One is of many colours, as if it had brushed up against a rainbow : the other is dead grey.

And yet on this question of colour one mustn't be too sweeping. I cannot forget the delightfully blue flagstones of a certain kitchen that I once knew, spotlessly clean after the constant washing.

The neighbours were always amazed to see how my mother could manage the process without dreaming of getting down on her knees ; and though she was certainly not slim and sylphlike, I think most gym. mistresses would envy her agility in stooping to wash the faces of those flagstones.

After supper it often happened that they again called for the ministry of soap and water, for now having been converted into a blue blackboard they were chalked over with geometrical figures.

It is a strange fact that the Euclid problem that had baffled me in black and white when printed small in my geometry book, became crystal clear as soon as my father had made a magnified copy in white and blue under my feet. In more senses than one I was now able to get right on top of it.

You will perhaps expect me to speak also about the iris flower which shares the name given to the fluttering square of canvas in the air and the stolid square of stone underfoot ; but I will not go after these gay "flags" of the garden and river edge, for I want to mention a " flag " that only Welsh people will recognise, and that with a broad grin.

When a South Walian refers to anybody as " an old flag " he has said the last word about him. I have never known why this poetic annexe should be added to the word's connotation, and I should not care to be challenged as to the exact definition of the significance of the term in this particular connection.

It casts no reflection on a man's moral character. It needn't of necessity mean that he is " airy-fairy", or too eager to be seen or showy, or indeed that he possesses any of the qualities that are usually associated with the article from which he borrows his name. Perhaps he is generally a bit foolish, a bit talkative, rather unpredictable and altogether undependable.

Neither can I say over what area this term is current coin, but here in South Wales whenever I have had occasion to pass it over the counter it is always accepted at its full value. You may be driven to think me a rogue, but even during this Coronation fever, please do not call me " an old flag " !

'The little envelopes'

"THAT isn't quite playing the game." Though my lips didn't frame the actual words, I said them loudly enough in my mind. And then I smiled.

A long-stalked, purplish flower was supposed to be growing right under a privet hedge that separated two little lawns. Its roots were counting on the soil of one lawn, but the flower itself bloomed above the neighbour lawn, having mischievously worked its way through the tangled hedge.

And I was smiling at such an exhibition of bad sportsmanship because it reminded me of what people said of Mari Blaengwernan when they discussed her Sunday loyalties. She attended Soar Chapel and took no little part in discussing the affairs of Soar and that with rare heat and eloquence, while as a matter of fact she had never brought her "letter" from Saron over the hill, and it was Saron that received her monthly contribution in the little envelopes, "*Y casis bach*."

And this is how one Saron woman summed up the position, going to the poultry run for her figure : "Mari does all her cackling in Soar, but she lays her eggs in Saron ! " ("*Mae Mari yn clochdar yn Soar ond yn dodwy yn Saron !*")

The *casis bach* (the little cases, or envelopes) helped to keep the smile on my face even after Mari Blaengwernan had left my mind.

In the country chapels of West Wales indulgence in strong drink, and drunkenness especially, is regarded as disloyalty to one's church membership. One poor fellow, a seafarer, who in this note may hide under the name of Lewys—Mari, Soar and Saron, too, wear their cloaks of pseudonymity—was often in trouble, but after each expulsion he was remorseful enough and humble enough to seek re-entrance to the fellowship.

The chapel hadn't a minister of its own, but it was often served by a preacher whose church was at no great distance. In the society meeting this minister had been asked to refer to Lewys, who was home from sea, and he said quite candidly that he was never altogether sure whether the poor in-and-out worshipper was a member or not at the moment.

Lewys's gruff reply from the back pew has almost become a classic—"*Rwy'n derbyn y casis bach yn regular !*" ("I get the little envelopes regularly!") Did he imply that the deacons were at any rate ready enough to accept his support, whether or not they accepted his company ?

It was at Ebenezer, though you may not find that name above the chapel door, that the minister was making an appeal for some good cause, and, to bring the matter home to the farming fraternity, pointing out that the half-a-crown per member that he was asking for was but the price of a chicken.

Among the minister's most loyal admirers was an old character whose words were few and very often enigmatic. When he arrived home his wife, who had not been to chapel, expected him to say something about the sermon, but all she had was a question on what was hardly a Sunday topic:

" What did you get for the fowls at the market on Friday ? "

" Two shillings. But why do you ask ? "

" He, in Ebenezer there, was getting half-crowns for them this morning."

And it was just like him to offer no further word of explanation. But I must explain to price-conscious housewives that all this happened a long time ago !

6th October, 1953

Moon-magic

THE " nine white nights of harvest "—" nawnos olau medi " have come and gone ; indeed the charmed short season was almost over before I had an opportunity of relishing to the full any of its moon-magic. It was only on one night that I found myself away from the town and out in a more or less open country where the view was unhampered. It had meant a short bus ride, and when I had stepped down and the bus had moved on I saw the full moon hanging low to my right.

I cannot say what was wrong, but that moon made no attempt to light up the sky or the earth. It was itself light enough, but it stood there in a sky that was as utterly black as the earth beneath it ; and that was how it had a chance to play a moment's trick with my imagination, for, before I knew it, I was looking not at the moon, but at the moon-face of Big Ben.

Did I say all was pitch black ? It certainly was, before I had seen the Westminster clock, but once I saw that lit clock-face the faint turreted outlines began to build themselves up, and for one moment I felt that I was actually standing on a London pavement, and it would have been the most natural thing in the world to have heard the pleasant chimes in the wind.

It was but for one moment, but I was grateful that some hours have their moments as well as their minutes.

Gypsy funeral

PENYFAI CHURCH is surely one of the most beautiful in the whole district, and one felt that no edifice could be too beautiful for the solemn gathering that came together there on a recent afternoon to pay tribute to the memory of one whose sterling character had made him the uncrowned king of those who prefer the freedom of tent and caravan to the walled and roofed homes of the masses.

He himself dwelt in a cottage, as did some of the mourners, but he had never lost his love for the open heath and the open sky. Before the funeral, as I turned to the twenty-third psalm in the very old Bible on the kitchen table, I realised how supremely fitting is this shepherd psalm on so many different occasions.

At funeral and wedding one turns to it instinctively, and in the Abbey and in the lowliest kitchen the word from the far Palestinian hills arrives to cheer and to heal.

" Crimond " may be heard too often to suit some musically sensitive ears but it is good to realise that a hymn-tune can become as popular as a piece of jazz and that at work and play men and women can joyfully tell the world that they count on a Shepherd.

I have listened to the tune sung in all sorts of buildings but it was only a few days ago that I was really deeply touched by it. I was hurrying past a local pop factory, or rather I failed to hurry past because of the whole-hearted strains of the psalm that soared above the hum of the machinery.

It was the " Kindly Light " hymn that the vicar gave out at Penyfai and under the robust leadership of a Welsh-speaking friend of the " king " we and the ninety mourners followed " o'er moor and fen " to the familiar strains of " Sandon."

13*th October*, 1953

At his finger-tips

IT was about time for the morning service to begin, and I could see that the young student sitting with me in the vestry was getting hot and nervous.

When at last I was on the point of opening the chapel door for him he took out his handkerchief and carefully wiped the fingers of both hands as you and I would have wiped our glasses.

He, too, wore glasses, but as they were there only to shield his eyes, it of course, mattered little whether they were misty or not ; his one concern was that there should be no blurring mist on his fingertips when he came to open the bulky Galatians that he carried under his left arm.

I hesitated for an instant at the foot of the pulpit steps, wondering whether I ought to offer to help him, for that top step was out of line with the edge of the pulpit floor, narrowing at one end almost to nothing and causing many a sighted divine to make a stumbling undignified entry. But I remembered that this was the student's second visit and that the foot of a blind man seldom forgets.

Almost before I had reached my pew he was giving out the opening hymn, whose number and first verse he had memorised. When he came to read the Lesson, I couldn't help thinking that he was making a tactical error in that he stood bolt upright, looking straight at the congregation, his fingers alone looking at the Braille.

Was it the fact that this was neither reciting nor yet reading that caused a kind of confusion in my mind ?

Old Mr. Davies, Capel y Glyn, the only blind preacher that I knew in my boyhood, was a far more cunning craftsman in this respect.

Because his finger-tips were also blind, for each service he had to commit to memory all four hymns together with the Scripture reading, but not a hymn did he give out without first picking up the pulpit book and finding the approximate number ; and as for the Lesson, after a few tentative approaches and some noisy leaf-turning he always arrived at the right chapter—or very near it.

Caught in the magic of his own play-acting he bent low over the Book as his eyes moved along the lines that he didn't see. And who will condemn a piece of sanctified guile that almost succeeded in removing a sense of embarrassing sympathy from a sensitive congregation ?

It was only once that Providence let him down. The few who sat in the gallery watched him reading one of the opening chapters of Matthew from the blank page between the two Testaments, and though they were not Church members they were relieved when the old prophet, after reading a few verses at the bottom of the page, turned over the cold, white leaf to continue on kindlier ground.

Once the sermon came he was free to forget the printed word and, of course, he disdained the use of " notes." There was no need for further make-believe, and to say that he soon warmed to his task is no mere figure of speech.

94

He had taken off his Inverness at the end of the reading and now as he introduces his sermon the second overcoat is divested. When he clomped into the church to open the service his breathing was a visible, rhythmic mist on the cold air ; now his fine head with its grey, hempen ringlets has its own halo of cloud.

No one blames him that he occasionally exceeds the orthodox allotted hour ; neither does anyone blame the milkmaids living in distant farms when they tip-toe their way to the door. If their shoes do not squeak they know that they can slip out undetected under the shadow of his great shouting.

The student's upright stance was all to the good when it came to the preaching, for the eyes that he counted on were on his manuscript while the eyes behind the glasses—those on which we counted—were directly on us, giving him an easy sense of confidence and giving us a feeling of being addressed directly and extemporaneously.

Did Davies y Glyn, even without his Braille, hold an advantage over the boy ? There would have been no need to ask such a question had you seen the old prophet in action, especially when both coats lay dead on the pulpit chair and his arms could move freely.

The student was allowed no such liberty for Louis Braille held on to him by his fingers. To him the dotted notes were essential, and so he could only speak with his tongue ; no wind of inspiration could fling his arms about ; passion could not rush into his hand and electrify a people with the touch of an out-stretched finger ; no argument could be clinched once and for all with the resounding note of hand on hand.

But then the blind preacher of Capel y Glyn had finished his last oration many years ago, and the student, too, has arrived, greatly relieved, at his quiet Amen, and as he came down those steps as unconcernedly as if every pulpit stairs that he had ever known had just that twist at the top, little did I think that I had heard him for the last time.

Edward Thorogood Kemp, the brilliant Hirwaun student died soon after being presented with his M.A. for a philosophy thesis.

20th October, 1953

The pensioner

A CARDIFF Scot often lamented the fact that we Southerners had given up using that most serviceable word " anent " ; wasn't it much neater than either " regarding " or " concerning," and preferable in every sort of way to that office-desk Latinism " re " ?

Well, then, anent the campaign against the "too old at 65" heresy, let me chronicle the story of a short conversation between myself and one who had called to have her pension paper signed. She had done excellent work, but rules are rules, and for some time now she had been superannuated.

My name having been duly inscribed, with the additional flourishes only to be expected of a fountain pen proudly conscious of belonging to a man described on the sheet as an "authorized person," I sat back to enjoy a chat. But no, she couldn't stay a moment for her father, who was working in the garden attending to the autumn tidying up, would be waiting for his tea.

" And how old is your father now ? "

" Eighty-six."

And now, anent nothing in the wide world, I must refer to an adventure that came to me on a recent dark night, an exciting adventure for me, although nothing happened.

The bus had stopped for a breather after climbing a hill, and I found that the girl conductor and I were the only people left in it, and with a smile she informed me that this was journey's end. She spoke impeccable Glamorgan Welsh, " terminus " being the only non-Welsh—non-English, too, for that matter—word that she used.

I had to take her word for it, but it was hard to believe that this sharp turn on the still climbing road was indeed the village to which I had booked.

I got out to see the bus manoeuvring into position for the return journey, and my eyes, gradually accustoming themselves to the dark, began to pick out certain forms and outlines.

There was no sign of a house anywhere, but gigantic shadow-shapes crowding round me told me that I was " in the hills." And there was something else.

On my right I made out incredibly high arches as if someone had thrown a bridge across from one cloud to another, and when I turned to the left there was its fellow, spanning two more clouds, just as high and just as incredible.

There was something fantastic about it all and I found it hard to believe that I was in Wales and not in some famed foreign land where man's soaring handiwork vies with nature at its extravagant best.

Of course the undreaming part of me knew where it was, and I guessed that a hundred yards further climb would bring me to Vanford Bridge. You will say that you have never heard of such a village in the Welsh hills, and I pray that you never will. I only introduce it to warn you of the kind of perpetration that may be one day effected by those who have no respect for genuine Welsh names.

Pontrhydyfen, the only name to which the village answers, is laden with local lore. The two magnificent bridges were not always there, but there was always a mountain track, and the creaking of the wain making for the ford along that track has come down through the ages, mellowed into music and chaliced forever, let us hope, in the syllables of Pontrhydyfen, one of the strongholds of Welsh culture.

27th October, 1953

" Seventy-three "

I HAVE often seen Tair Gwaith stamped on the foreheads of careering motor-buses but as a rule they speeded by so swiftly that I missed the all important apostrophe between two letters, the omission of which was enough to convert " the Work's houses " (" Tai'r Gwaith ") into a bit of the multiplication table—" Three times " (" Tair gwaith ").

This mathematical fragment reminded me of how a popular character in a certain valley had to be satisfied with a number instead of a name.

He was referred to as " 73," or so it sounded ; and the story of the name is a rather complicated one.

Know in the first place that our hero lived in one of a tiny row of houses ; three to be exact. The row hadn't a proper name but was simply known as " Tri thy " (" Three houses ").

Samuel to the men of the valley was Sam Tri thy, which soon jumbled itself up into Sam Ty three, and then the inevitable Seventy-three, and so it was that a respectable citizen who had never seen the inside of prison had to answer to a number all the days of his life.

3rd November, 1953

Pencil-marks

LAST August, when all good Welshmen were at the Eisteddfod, I was standing and staring at a second-hand bookshop in Aberystwyth. There was a slim volume, " W. H. Davies, Poems 1930-1931," and on my way out, standing on the step between shop and pavement, I opened the book at a page which had been marked by the previous owner.

His pencil called my eyes to these lines :—
An old dog friend—*whose kennel was my shadow*
Has left it empty, and I feel the cold.

It may be sacrilege to mention money in such connections, but in common parlance I had already received my money's worth. How many pages of Eisteddfod transactions would one have to trudge through before coming across such lines, and not only these competitive poems—one mentions the Eisteddfod solely because it happens to be August—but so·many compositions in Welsh and English where the ideas, when at last unravelled, are far from being fresh.

My unknown friend of the pencil—I wish I knew who he was —has only one other mark of approbation, and I quote what he has marked as the verse happens to disabuse the mind of any critic who imagines that these bits of perfection came to Davies easily and inevitably.

He has spoken of the Night " flustered at having all those jewels there," spilling her stars, " as though she carried more than she could bear."

 " While I, a struggling dreamer, all day long,
  That tries to polish one poor little rhyme,
  Though breathed on hard and rubbed with ecstasy,
  Still call on Night to see my wasted time."

The only other pencil mark was one of surprised disapproval linking together two words, " leave " and " breathe," which the poet had accepted as rhymes. While not justifying W. H. Davies, I might note perhaps that to-day's poets would probably cavil at " leave, breathe," not because it is only a near rhyme but on account of the fact that it is a too near rhyme. They make it a matter of literary conscience to discover pairs that can only hang together by the skin of their teeth.

This is Louis MacNeice :—

 " Having bitten on life like a sharp apple
 Or, playing it like a fish, been happy,
 Having felt with fingers that the sky is blue
 What have we after that to look forward to ?
 Not the twilight of the gods but a precise dawn
 Of sallow and grey bricks, and newsboys crying war."

He must have kicked himself when he noticed the dated " blue, to," that he had perpetrated !

It is a pity that Wilfred Owen, true poet that he was, should be to-day remembered, especially in classrooms, because of his rhyming innovations. But he worked to a plan, and whether he himself realised it or not it was a plan that was related more or less to one of the orthodox methods of Welsh rhyming.

His closing consonants tally while the vowels vary :—

> "Watching, we hear the mad gusts tugging on the wire,
>   Like twitching agonies of men among its brambles.
>   Northward, incessantly, the flickering gunnery rumbles,
> Far off, like a dull rumour of some other war.
>   What are we doing here ? "

Years ago I remember reading in translation a Russian poem, where the poet addresses his ink-well and recalls the time he had spent in seeking for the ends of lines in its black depths.

As a rule the rhymes we fish for are certainly " the end of lines," but occasionally they turn up at the middle of lines, too, and on one occasion I remember how surprised I was to find them claiming " first priority " (what a phrase !) at the beginning.

It was a schoolboy who brought his attempt to me when I found that all his lines ended without any suggestion of rhyming while the openings rhymed perfectly. When I asked him why, I was met by his ready " Why not ? " He had stolen a march on many modernists.